LIGHT IN AUGUST

A Study in Black and White

TWAYNE'S MASTERWORK STUDIES

Robert Lecker, General Editor

LIGHT IN AUGUST

A Study in Black and White

Alwyn Berland

TWAYNE PUBLISHERS • NEW YORK
Maxwell Macmillan Canada • Toronto
Maxwell Macmillan International • New York   Oxford   Singapore   Sydney

"Nobel Prize Acceptance Speech." From *Essays, Speeches, and Public Letters* by William Faulkner.
Copyright © 1965 by Random House, Inc.
Reprinted by permission of Random House, Inc.

Twayne's Masterwork Studies No. 95

Light in August: A Study in Black and White
Alwyn Berland

Twayne Publishers
Macmillan Publishing Company
866 Third Avenue
New York, New York 10022

Maxwell Macmillan Canada, Inc.
1200 Eglinton Avenue East
Suite 200
Don Mills, Ontario M3C 3N1

Library of Congress Cataloging-in-Publication Data

Berland, Alwyn.
    Light in August : a study in black and white / Alwyn Berland.
        p.   cm. — (Twayne's masterwork studies ; no. 95)
    Includes bibliographical references and index.
    ISBN 0-8057-8050-5 (alk. paper). — ISBN 0-8057-8100-5 (pbk. : alk. paper)
    1. Faulkner, William, 1897–1962.   Light in August.   2. Light and darkness in literature.   I. Title.   II. Series.
PS3511.A86L5714   1992
813'.52—dc20
                                                            92-28709
                                                            CIP

The paper used in this publication meets the minimum requirements of American National Standard for Information Sciences—Permanence of Paper for Printed Library Materials. ANSI Z3948-1984. ∞™

10 9 8 7 6 5 4 3 2 1 (hc)
10 9 8 7 6 5 4 3 2 1 (pb)

Printed in the United States of America

CONTENTS

NOTE ON THE REFERENCES
AND ACKNOWLEDGMENTS

I have quoted in this study from the readily available Modern Library College Edition of *Light in August* (1968). Its text is reproduced photographically from the first printing of the novel in October 1932.

Some of my understanding of and enthusiasm for *Light in August* was recorded as early as 1962 in a published article. Since that time my understanding has expanded and been refined, but not substantially changed. The number of books and articles that others have written about Faulkner subsequently is legion; a comprehensive bibliography of secondary sources on *Light in August* alone must be daunting to any student or would-be critic, although the tenure and promotions committee that sits at the pearly gates would not judge all of this material of equal value. I am indebted to many works that have preceded this one; specific debts are acknowledged in the Notes and References. In addition to these, I have been impressed with a number of critical studies of Faulkner's work—among them those by Malcolm Cowley, Irving Howe, and Michael Millgate—which are listed in the Selected Bibliography at the end of this volume. And every student of Faulkner must give special acknowledgment to Joseph Blotner for his comprehensive and judicious two-volume *Faulkner: A Bibliography* (New York: Random House, 1974).

I would also like to acknowledge a grant from the Arts Research Board of McMaster University, which made some travel possible; and the cooperation I received from the librarians of the Faulkner Collections at the University of Virginia and the University of Mississippi. I am grateful to some of my graduate students at McMaster

University both for their own perceptive readings of Faulkner and for their alert skepticism toward the soft places in my developing ideas.

Finally, I wish to thank my wife, Jayne Berland, some of whose own ideas about Faulkner I have shamelessly plagiarized. Her patient skill as an editor has on occasion driven me to fury, but once past that, to gratitude and admiration.

For Jayne

. . . sing whatever is well made

William Faulkner
Photograph courtesy of Jill Faulkner Summers.

CHRONOLOGY: WILLIAM WILLIAM FAULKER'S LIFE AND WORKS

1825   Great-grandfather, William Clark Falkner, "The Old Colonel," Civil War veteran, railway builder, author of the popular *The White Rose of Memphis* (1881), born in Knox County, Tennessee. Model for the Colonel Sartoris of Faulkner's fiction.

1870   Father, Murry Cuthbert Falkner, born in Ripley, Mississippi.

1871   Mother, Maud Butler, born.

1889   W. C. Falkner shot and killed by Richard Thurmond, his former partner.

1896   Murry Falkner and Maud Butler married.

1897   William Cuthbert Falkner born in New Albany, Mississippi, 25 September. (He will later add *u* to family name, and it is as William Faulkner that he will be known.)

1898   Family moves to Ripley.

1902   Murry Falkner moves family to Oxford, Mississippi, which becomes the model for Faulkner's fictional "Jefferson." Murry works at a number of jobs, including 10 years as business manager at the University of Mississippi. Regarded as a good man, but rather weak and ineffectual; may explain why Faulkner's imaginative paternity goes back to his great-grandfather, and why his fiction frequently concerns theme of family decline.

1905   William Faulkner begins first grade.

1914   Quits school, after some years of dwindling interest. (Will go back the following year, only to quit again.) Meets Phil Stone, an Oxford lawyer, who encourages Faulkner's literary ambitions over the years. Faulkner's fictional character, Gavin Stevens, partly based on Stone. During this period he poses as aesthete and dandy; earns local epithet "Count No-Count." His life-long habit of drinking begins.

1918   Estelle Oldham, with whom Faulkner was in love, announces her engagement to Cornell Franklin, whom she marries in April. Faulkner tries to enlist in armed services, but is rejected. Changes name from Falkner to Faulkner, and in July, using bogus papers, enlists in the Royal Canadian Air Force as an Englishman. Posted to training in Toronto. (Later there develops a legend—one of many that Faulkner's life inspires—that he joined the R.A.F. because he refused to fight with the "Damn Yankees." In truth, he joined the R.A.F. because he was too short and frail to meet the standards of the American Air Force.) World War I ends on 11 November, while he is still training; Faulkner returns to Oxford in December.

1919   First published poem appears in the *New Republic*. Enrolls as a veteran at the University of Mississippi ("Ole Miss"). Publishes poems and drawings in student publications. The University is in Oxford in Faulkner's fiction, at a site near the fictional Jefferson, as in *Sanctuary*.

1920   Quits university, but continues with student drama group, for which he writes a verse play, *Marionettes*.

1921   Leaves for New York, with encouragement of Stark Young, an established Southern writer. Works in bookstore. Returns to Oxford in December, takes job as university postmaster, and serves as voluntary scoutmaster.

1924   Removed as scoutmaster, probably as result of drinking, and resigns as postmaster. His first volume of poetry, *The Marble Faun*, published by Four Seas Co. for which Faulkner must pay a subsidy of $400.

1925   Meets distinguished author Sherwood Anderson in New Orleans. Begins work on a novel. Travels in Italy, Switzerland, and France. Stays on Left Bank in Paris. Despite the popular expatriate movement, made famous by such writers as Ernest Hemingway and Gertrude Stein, Faulkner leaves Paris in December and returns to Oxford, Mississippi.

1926   *Soldier's Pay*, Faulkner's first novel, published by Boni and Liveright.

1927   Second novel, *Mosquitoes*, published by Liveright. Horace Liveright rejects manuscript of *Flags in the Dust*, a long novel about the Sartoris family.

1928   Works on *The Sound and the Fury*. Harcourt, Brace accepts manuscript of *Sartoris*, a revised and shortened version of *Flags in the Dust*.

1929   *Sartoris* published; first novel in which Faulkner finds his major subject, the fictional history of Yoknapatawpha County. Estelle Oldham Franklin is divorced, after some unhappy years. In June, Faulkner marries Estelle. *The Sound and the Fury* is published by Jonathan Cape & Harrison Smith. During this period he completes first version of *Sanctuary*, and begins *As I Lay Dying*.

1930　Buys antebellum house, which he names "Rowan Oak," in Oxford. ("Rowan Oak" is now maintained as Faulkner Museum.) National magazines begin buying his short stories. *As I Lay Dying* published.

1931　First child, Alabama Faulkner, born, but lives only nine days. *Sanctuary* published. Feverish re-writing following acceptance of manuscript. Novel has scandalous reception. First short-story collection, *These Thirteen*, published.

1932　Short of money, despite remarkable productivity and publication success. Begins first job in Hollywood as script writer; irregular periods of movie work occupy him for many years. Father, Murry Falkner, dies. *Light in August* published.

1933　Second volume of poetry, *A Green Bough*, published. Daughter, Jill Faulkner, born in June. Faulkner takes flying lessons, buys an airplane.

1934　Second short-story collection, *Doctor Martino and Other Stories*, published. Begins work on *Absalom, Absalom!*

1935　*Pylon* is published. Writes several stories later incorporated into *The Unvanquished*. Begins first of several affairs with women in Hollywood.

1936　Spends much of year in Hollywood; Estelle and Jill with him for a month. *Absalom, Absalom!* published by Random House.

1938　*The Unvanquished* published; screen rights purchased by M.G.M. Buys a farm, which he names "Greenfield Farm"; purchase increases financial pressures on Faulkner.

1939　Elected to the National Institute of Arts and Letters. *The Wild Palms* published.

1940　Caroline Barr, Faulkner family servant and author's "Mammy," dies. *The Hamlet* published. First major study of Snopes clan, which later will be expanded to a trilogy.

1941　Works on *Go Down, Moses*. Organizes wartime aircraft warning system in his county.

1942　*Go Down, Moses* published; dedication is to Caroline Barr. Begins five-month assignment with Warner Brothers in Hollywood.

1943   In Hollywood again, for seven months' work. Begins work on manuscript that many years later will be published as *A Fable*.

1944   Returns to Hollywood for long stay; Estelle and Jill with him for two months. Begins long correspondence with Malcolm Cowley, who is working on Viking Portable selection of Faulkner's work.

1946   *The Portable Faulkner*, with influential introduction by Malcolm Cowley, published.

1947   The *Partisan Review* rejects "Notes on a Horse-Thief," a portion of *A Fable* in progress.

1948   U.S. Supreme Court in a historic ruling decrees that federal and state courts cannot enforce restrictive covenants that bar persons from owning or occupying property because of race. *Intruder in the Dust* published. First novel by Faulkner to win wide popularity, in part because of national prominence of racial issues. Faulkner elected to American Academy of Arts and Letters. Now a "famous" contemporary writer. There is, however, considerable resentment of Faulkner in the South because of his tempered stand on racial integration.

1949   Involved with preparations for filming of *Intruder in the Dust*. *Knight's Gambit* (collection of short stories) published.

1950   *Collected Stories of William Faulkner* published. Goes to Stockholm with daughter Jill to receive Nobel Prize for Literature. Delivers the now-famous Nobel Prize acceptance speech.

1951   Several years of travel in United States and Europe to receive new honors and awards, and to work on film projects, and to consult about staging *Requiem for a Nun*. *Requiem for a Nun* published.

1954   U.S. Supreme Court declares segregation in public schools unconstitutional. *A Fable* published. Attends International Writers' Conference in São Paulo. Daughter Jill marries Paul D. Summers. Faulkner continues to travel, sometimes on behalf of U.S. State Department, and spends extended periods in New York.

1955   National Book Award for *A Fable*. Pulitzer Prize for Fiction. Travels to Japan, Europe, and Iceland for State Department. Involvement with issues of racial integration deepens, following important Supreme Court rulings. *Big Woods* published. Rosa Parks's arrest for refusing to give up her bus seat to a white man in Montgomery, Alabama, touches off famous bus boycott by blacks. Martin Luther King, Jr., elected chairman of boycott organization, becoming prominent spokesman on racial issues.

CHRONOLOGY

1956	Writes articles on integration. Visits Charlottesville, Virginia, where, in April, his grandson is born.
1957	Begins semester as writer-in-residence at the University of Virginia. *The Town*, a sequel to *The Hamlet*, published. President orders federal troops to Little Rock, Arkansas, to prevent interference with school integration at Central High School.
1958	Second term as writer-in-residence at the University of Virginia; then two weeks at Princeton for Council on Humanities.
1959	American stage debut of *Requiem for a Nun* at the Golden Theater, New York, receives mainly poor critical reviews. (There had been an earlier and highly acclaimed London production under the direction of the distinguished Tony Richardson.) Motion picture version of *The Sound and the Fury* opens. Faulkner receives offer for film rights for *Light in August*. (Film was never produced.) Attends UNESCO conference in Denver. Third volume of trilogy, *The Mansion*, published.
1960	Bequeaths manuscripts to William Faulkner Foundation. (These are at the University of Virginia; other papers and manuscripts are at the University of Mississippi and the University of Texas.)
1961	Goes to Venezuela for two weeks for State Department.
1962	Visiting Writer at U.S. Military Academy at West Point. Accepts Gold Medal for Fiction from the National Institute of Arts and Letters. Faulkner's last novel, *The Reivers*, published. In poor health, resulting partly from falls while horseback riding. Has bouts of very heavy drinking, which require occasional hospitalization. On 5 July enters a clinic near Oxford. Dies of heart failure on 6 July, in his sixty-fourth year. Buried in St. Peter's Cemetery, Oxford, the next day.

LITERARY AND HISTORICAL CONTEXT

1

Historical Context

William Faulkner is now acknowledged to be one of the great writers not only of the twentieth-century American novel but of modern literature generally. Awarded the Nobel Prize for Literature in 1950, his work is well known and admired throughout the world. Although his greatest works were written over fifty years ago, his work can still be thought of by many students and general readers as too experimental in form, and too "difficult" in meaning. It may be helpful, therefore, to discuss Faulkner in the context of modern literature.

The twentieth-century has been marked by unprecedented experimentation and change in the arts. Movements in music, painting, sculpture, and literature have broken with convention and tradition to attempt new forms and new methods. Many of these movements are associated with the term *modernism*, as well as a number of particular modernist schools, or submovements. For all its range and variety, the single dominating feature of modernism, and its frequent battle cry, was Ezra Pound's demand, "MAKE IT NEW!" As a result, more artistic experimentation and innovation have taken place than in any other period in the past. Not only artistic forms and traditions, but also religious, social, moral, and political beliefs have been challenged, questioned, or, more recently, simply ignored.

It could be argued that modern technology makes for social discontinuity. In a technological age discontinuity is an inherent, perhaps even deliberately sought-after, quality. There is a confused notion of progress which holds that new is better. In the work of Faulkner, the divisive pull of the historical sense shared by the traditional American South, on the one hand, and the modern world's flight from history on the other, created a particularly strong tension.

In poetry, we have seen the virtual abandonment of traditional poetic form and structure; a new poetry of free verse without rhyme or regular meter, a poetry of private symbolism such as T. S. Eliot's early poetry, or Ezra Pound's cantos. Typographical experiments abandon capital letters and most punctuation, as in the poetry of e e cummings, and "sound" poetry where the poet chants repeated consonants or vowels.

Readers of the novel, accustomed to the narrative traditions of great Victorian novelists such as Dickens or Hardy, are in for a surprise when they turn to James Joyce, Virginia Woolf, or William Faulkner.

One result of all this experimentation and discontinuity is that people sometimes feel confused by modern artistic expression. Not surprisingly, many wonder why the modern arts should be so "unorthodox," so challenging, so difficult. Perhaps all of these changes could be attributed simply to the desire for innovation and change, for novelty, or even for shock value. But these are symptoms, I believe, and must not be mistaken for causes.

There has been rapid change and progress in almost every form of knowledge and discourse. Perhaps more immediately important to the subject of literature, however, are the drastic changes in the ways we think about human beings: their place in the world, the object or purpose of human existence, the nature of death. Western civilization developed for many centuries with a more or less commonly shared worldview—a basic agreement about the world as a creation of God, about human beings having manifest moral and ethical obligations. The modern world no longer holds these views with any commonality, nor has it produced any others that command universal loyalty.

Men and women are made in God's image, or are the psychologists' rats in a maze—perhaps complex rats with more circuits and a maze with more trapdoors. Human conduct is measured by some objective morality—or by completely relativistic prohibitions imposed by self-interested cultures or power elites. Our conduct shapes the world we live in—or the end justifies the means, and conduct doesn't matter so long as our goals satisfy us. Human life *has* a goal (choose one)—or it has no particular point or destination, human life being accident or spectacle without ultimate meaning. We live for salvation, or for progress, or for domination, or for a guaranteed annual income, preferably tax free.

The modern world has called into question not only traditional systems of belief, but also traditional ways of seeing and thinking, traditional ways of understanding and of portraying human thought and conduct. Traditional art forms have changed correspondingly. In the novel, such changes include: the development of "stream of consciousness" characterization and narrative (so brilliantly displayed in Faulkner's *The Sound and the Fury*), experimentation in time sequences and chronology (as in *Sound and Fury* and, to a degree, *Light in August*), and deliberate ambiguity of meaning.

The traditional novel reflected the assumption that we can completely know an objective reality, and understand human actions and their causes and effects. It was assumed that the novelist had these issues under firm control. These certainties were reflected in the ordered shaping of plots. The creation of a sense of organic unity in the work of art might be said to derive from the sense of control the artist has over the material of life. Even in novels with many plots and subplots, such as Dickens's *Bleak House*, narrative strands are ultimately woven together to create the sense of a unified world understood and controlled by the author. The "artfulness" of art in the well-crafted novel, such as Henry James's *The Ambassadors*, is the careful structuring that attempts to give order to the apparent diffuseness of life. The artfulness of art in Faulkner is the careful structuring that attempts to convey the basic uncertainty and ambiguity of life through exploiting the relativity of different points of view, and through a variety of styles and narrative techniques all within the same novel.

Light in August does not present a world whose total coherence is reflected in authorial certainty or traditionally unified form. It dramatizes ambiguities and inconclusiveness. The significance of many aspects of the story may be uncertain, or interpreted in different ways. Varied, perhaps even contradictory, interpretations are left to the reader. Faulkner is the inventor and author of the characters in *Light in August,* as well as of its setting and its actions. He might well assume a total understanding and control of them. But there are strange ambiguities in the novel. Does Joe Christmas kill his foster father? Why does Joe Christmas murder Joanna Burden instead of simply leaving her? Who sets fire to her house? Does Gail Hightower die in the novel? Why do we never learn the truth about Joe Christmas's parentage and his color? Some contradictions in chronology and time are no doubt the result of carelessness in writing and revision, but do not some of these problems reflect the uncertainties that cut across our claims of absolute knowledge?

●　　●　　●

The modern novelist is not free to draw on a common worldview or on a value system shared with his readers; he is, rather, challenged to create a value system within his own work, and to give it substance in the lives of his characters. Faulkner has done this in a remarkably sustained way through his invention of Yoknapatawpha County. It is inhabited by generations of fictional characters, who came to Mississippi and bought land, or gambled for it, or simply took it. His narratives follow the development of the plantation and slave economy, the Civil War and its aftermath, and the evolution of the modern South.

Faulkner published a number of novels and short stories in which he invested his characters with an intense and vivid sense of reality, and gave them a significance that goes far beyond their lives in a particular time and place. More than any other American novelist of the twentieth century, he has dealt directly with the largest human dilemmas: What gives value and worth to human life? Why, and for what, do human beings strive? What is the nature of virtue? of evil?

What are the limits of human freedom? No other American novelist in our century has done so much to expand the scope of fiction both in its artistic and thematic possibilities.

• • •

It remains for us to consider Faulkner's relationship to the literature of the American South. If discontinuity is characteristic of Faulkner's modernism, it also plays a part in his relationship to the literature of his region. But there are continuities as well, stemming from a shared culture, and a mythologizing of this culture intensified by the Civil War and the defeat of the South.

Southern antebellum novels were mainly romances, heavily influenced by the fiction of Sir Walter Scott and, to a lesser degree, James Fenimore Cooper. In these novels there is frequently a self-conscious insistence on the distinctive qualities of the South. These characteristics are associated with the aristocratic traditions of the English Cavaliers, in contrast with the materialism of the North. Frequently these novels include some justification or rationalization of slavery. No major Southern novelist emerged, although one, William Gilmore Simms, had a substantial reputation in the nineteenth century.

A different kind of writer, Edgar Allan Poe, was born in Baltimore and spent most of his formative years in the South, mainly in Virginia. Developing from "internationalist" rather than native literary sources and inspirations, he thrilled many generations of international readers with his intensity and his high Gothic flame in stories of terror, several brilliant tales based on exact reasoning, and a body of poetry mainly dark in tone, dismal in theme, and mechanical in metrics. It is debatable whether Poe influenced Faulkner in any marked way—still,—one thinks of the strong Gothic elements in such stories as "A Rose for Emily." Perhaps they simply had some temperamental similiarities as well as shared cultural traditions.

After the Civil War, realism came more and more to dominate American literature. In the South, George Washington Cable wrote some fine local-color stories about the Creoles of Louisiana, as well as what has been called the first realistic Southern novel, *The Grandissimes* (1880). Any reader of Faulkner will recognize Cable's sympathy for, and identification with, the Old South, which goes hand in hand with the painful judgment of its evils—especially slavery.

Cable, as well as later local-color and realist writers, delighted in recording, or creating the illusion of, vernacular language: local dialects and the idioms of Creoles and blacks and hill people. A similar impulse informed the writing of southern and southwestern humorists such as Longstreet, Thompson, and Hooper, even before the Civil War. After the war this tradition was elevated to brilliance by G. W. Harris in the Sut Lovingood yarns published in 1867. They had a great influence on the work of the greatest writer in this tradition, Mark Twain. One can trace this important element of Southern literature further, not only in Faulkner, but in such writers as Erskine Caldwell, Eudora Welty, Flannery O'Connor, and Ernest J. Gaines.

Faulkner shared with other writers of his region an intense feeling for the land as well as for its romantic and tragic history, and a strong identification with the South as a geographical place. Southern writers were aware of a common value system. This value system contained many contradictions that might cause doubt and ambivalence, but it inspired a basic loyalty at the same time. These affinities are more important in considering Faulkner's fiction than any strong literary infuences coming from earlier Southern writers.

I have commented on what I believe is a literary tradition from which Faulkner benefited and which he carried forward in a masterful way: the Southern tradition of vernacular humor. But in the wider scope of his writing—its historical sweep, its tragic intensity, its craftsmanship, and its daring formal and technical qualities—one sees less a Southern influence than a schooling in the great masters of prose fiction, such as Balzac, Dostoevsky, Conrad, and Joyce.

The late 1920s marked the beginning of an important renaissance in Southern literature. In 1929, Faulkner published his first breakthrough novel, *Sartoris*, and what is probably his most famous novel, *The Sound and the Fury*. In the same year, Thomas Wolfe published his first novel, *Look Homeward, Angel*, to launch a career that for many years was more widely known and admired than Faulkner's. First novels were published in 1929 also by Erskine Caldwell and Robert Penn Warren, among others. Soon after came the impressive short stories of Katherine Anne Porter, and a little later those of Eudora Welty. The Fugitive group staked out a strong Southern identity, and John Crowe Ransom and Allen Tate emerged as important poets, followed by Robert Penn Warren, and John Peale Bishop. Then came Randall Jarrell and, in time, James Dickey. A number of black writers made their mark, including Countee Cullen, Jean Toomer, Anne Spencer, James Weldon Johnson, and Langston Hughes.

Later still, the ongoing southern renaissance saw the emergence of a remarkable line of writers, white and black, including Richard Wright, Truman Capote, Walker Percy, William Styron, Flannery O'Connor, Carson McCullers, John Barth, James Baldwin, Ralph Ellison, and Ernest J. Gaines. It can be said that most of these writers wrote with a great awareness of William Faulkner, although with varying degrees of direct influence. A later generation of black writers, including Zora Neale Hurston, Alice Walker, Toni Morrison, and Bobbie Ann Mason, writes fiction that seems less affected by the powerful reach of Faulkner's Yoknapatawpha County. Still, Faulkner's fiction remains the most ambitious and most fully realized art that has ever emerged from the American South.

2

The Importance of the Work

In *Light in August* Faulkner undertook the difficult task of dealing with many of the complex and painful issues of our time: race relations in the American South, the burdens of repressive cultural and religious traditions, and with the modern theme of alienation—the loss of personal identity, of community, of rootedness. He dramatized, in a powerful way, the tragic nature of violence, not only the violence of individuals, but also the violence that can issue from society and from fixed and dogmatic systems of belief.

He did not deal with these powerful and urgent themes in the narrow tradition of documentary realism, nor yet as fiction-coated sociology. Instead, they are elevated to a kind of universal significance and worth by the author's particular genius. What is most memorable in Faulkner's fiction, besides its technical virtuosity and craftsmanship, is his vision. I mean by this not only the scope and range of his fiction, but also his desire and ability to deal with the largest human themes.

Faulkner wrote his greatest work in a period dominated by the emergence of Hemingway, and of other writers excessively suspicious of large themes, or of ambitious claims about human aspiration. The atmosphere of disillusionment that set in after World War I influenced such works as Hemingway's short-story collection *In Our Time* (1925), and his very successful novels *The Sun Also Rises* (1926) and *A Farewell to Arms* (1929). The Hemingway style—spare, emotionally restrained, stoically avoiding complex sentences as well as large aspirations—was thought to mirror the reality of human life. Some of this postwar disenchantment can be seen also in Faulkner's first novel, *Soldier's Pay* (1926). Going against the temper of his time, Faulkner went far beyond this stoical resistance to human striving, as well as to any rhetoric in style. In his very moving acceptance speech for the Nobel Prize in 1950 (which is reproduced as an appendix to this study), he insisted that the task of the writer is to treat the largest, and most permanent and universal of human themes: "love and honor and pity and pride and compassion and sacrifice." The writer who does not, he claimed, "labors under a curse. He writes not of love but of lust, of defeats in which nobody loses anything of value, of victories without hope, and worst of all, without pity or compassion."

There is something daring and magnanimous in staking out such claims for fiction in an age dominated by more narrow views of human possibility. These would include literary naturalism, with its emphasis on determinism, and its tendency to see all human conduct as bound by the stimuli and responses of behaviorism.

That Faulkner attempted such large human themes with so much literary imagination and craft in a historical period of skepticism and diminution may explain in large measure why it took so long for the general public to recognize his fiction. It may explain as well why Faulkner's works are now seen as a major accomplishment in the history of American literature and as great achievements in the fiction of our century.

• • •

The prodigality of Faulkner's imagination is evidenced not only in his range of structural and stylistic accomplishments, but also in the richness and sheer quantity of his fiction. He is the author of some 20 novels and a large body of short fiction. Among the major authors of

American literature, only Henry James was as prolific. Faulkner also wrote a number of "commercial" short stories when he needed money, and gave perhaps too much of his time and energy to his Hollywood scriptwriting. Certainly no one would claim that all of his novels achieve the high mastery of his best work. But even after all of these allowances, it is still the case that he created an impressively large body of major work that is difficult to match in twentieth-century Western literature.

A further distinction of Faulkner's work is in its grand design. Faulkner created an entire fictional landscape, Yoknapatawpha County, teeming with characters from every walk of life: pre–Civil War landed gentry, merchants and professionals, prosperous farmers and rednecks, black slaves and Indians, gamblers and gangsters, gentle-women and country girls and prostitutes. Perhaps he was inspired by the example of Balzac, a novelist whom Faulkner particularly admired and respected, who had created the vast *La Comedie Humaine*, a series of interrelated novels that had the ambitious aim of recording the entirety of nineteenth-century French society. Like Balzac, Faulkner created a series of novels, many of them involving characters present in other works, that made up a kind of legendary history of Yoknapatawpha County from the time of the Indians to the present day.

One should consider also the sheer prodigality of Faulkner's gift as a storyteller. He invented countless narratives, wonderful *stories*—comic, tragic, fabulous. Stemming perhaps in part from a Southern oral tradition of storytelling, in part from his extremely wide reading, but mainly from his own talent, he has the supreme ability to grip us with his stories, to keep us reading. The British novelist E. M. Forster once wrote that the basic objective of all narrative is to make us eager to know "And then?—And then?" While some readers might complain that Faulkner can be a difficult writer, few can complain that he is an uninteresting one.

•   •   •

The fictional world that Faulkner created is inhabited by a substantial cast of characters, a very large number of whom are developed in a major way. They are characters of three-dimensional solidity who—in a favorite expression of Faulkner's—"cast a shadow." Indeed, it was difficult for Faulkner to introduce a character into his fiction without inventing a full biography for him or her. One well-known example relates to *The Sound and the Fury*. Many years after the publication of this novel, Malcolm Cowley asked Faulkner for some background information that might be useful to readers of the anthology that Cowley was preparing (*The Portable Faulkner*). Faulkner sent back a remarkable set of biographies, which have since been published as an appendix to later editions of the novel. This appendix now seems to most contemporary readers an integral part of *The Sound and the Fury*. What is so striking about it is the way that Faulkner, many years after writing and publishing the novel, begins again to invent fuller lives for a number of its characters, even some who do not actually appear in the novel. While the novel was published in 1929, the life of Caddy Compson is carried forward to about 1940, in a way that makes her story in the novel itself even more poignant.

Evidence of this fecundity can be found in *Light in August* as well. Not only are a number of stories created in this novel, but each of them becomes richly elaborated. Faulkner not only introduces a character in the present, such as Joanna Burden, but also invests her with several generations of antecedents, whose own stories are related with great vividness. They may or may not be directly germane to the story of Joe Christmas, but Calvin and Nathaniel Burden and their families take on memorable life; we remember them long after we may have forgotten their particular roles in the novel. Similarly, the ghosts of Gail Hightower's past are created with great detail: grandfather, father, black servant, young bride all take on a solid reality far beyond any requirement that the novel's story imposes upon them. We are not given a simple expository account of how Joe Christmas's "real" father came to be killed, but rather a full and vividly created scene, almost as though this were a major element of the novel. The same may be said of the entire episode that leads to Joe's attack on his foster father, McEachern. This illustrates that almost nothing touches Faulkner's imagination that is not transformed into rich fictional representation.

3

Critical Reception

As with many other aspects of Faulkner's career, a good deal of legend has been generated about the reputation of his fiction among critics and readers before he was awarded the Nobel Prize for Literature in 1950.

Legend has it that Faulkner was totally neglected by critics and insufficiently appreciated by book-buying readers at least until 1948, when the publication of *Intruder in the Dust* generated very lively interest. *Sanctuary* did enjoy a kind of succès de scandale, and led to one of the first movies made from a Faulkner work, as *The Story of Temple Drake* (1933). Indeed, Faulkner claimed—with the untrustworthiness that accompanied many of his public pronouncements— that the writing of this rather sensational and violent novel had been motivated by his impatience with the meager sales of his earlier works. Given the legends, it might be useful to review the general development of Faulkner's reputation as a writer before turning to a consideration of the critical reception of *Light in August*.

While Faulkner certainly had an appreciative following during the earlier years of his career, it was apparently insufficient to generate an adequate income. His reputation, if not his sales, was impressive enough to lead various Hollywood studios to offer him contracts as a scriptwriter, with the accompanying hazards of time and increasing alcohol consumption and distraction from his real ambitions as a serious novelist. Many of the novels and stories that Faulkner wrote from the late 1920s until at least 1942 have come to be regarded as modern classics. Most of his fiction, however, was unavailable in bookstores by around the mid-1940s.

My own personal experience provides a good example of the accessibility of Faulkner's work in the 1940s. I was charged in about 1947 with the task of checking and supplementing the library's collection of modern American literature at a large and reputable Midwestern university. The number of Faulkner's titles on hand was lamentably small. Even worse, most of Faulkner's books were out of print at his American publishers, and therefore unavailable for purchase, unless one combed used-book stores. Curiously, many of his books were still in print and available through Faulkner's English publisher, Chatto & Windus. In consequence, this Midwestern university for many years represented one of America's most distinguished writers by way of English editions.

By the 1940s Faulkner was considered a kind of "novelist's novelist"—a writer whose technique and craft were exceptional. But he lacked the wider visibility that had been accorded to many of his contemporaries, such as Hemingway, Lewis, and Fitzgerald. A bibliographic reference work lists 24 articles on Faulkner for the year 1933, most of them occasional reviews of individual novels or poetry. By 1948 the number had risen only to 28, but these include some serious studies in literary magazines. By 1951, the year following his Nobel Prize award, two books and some 64 reviews and articles were published on Faulkner. The number of books and articles would increase steadily thereafter. The earliest close analysis of a Faulkner novel had been published in 1935.[1] A well-known "little magazine," *Perspective*, devoted a whole issue to articles on Faulkner in 1949, and another in 1950. But the first book-length study of Faulkner did not appear until 1951.[2]

Ironically, Faulkner's reputation grew more rapidly in France.[3]

Three of France's most eminent novelists—Andre Malraux, Jean-Paul Sartre, and Albert Camus—wrote about his work, and a number of French critics later produced excellent critical studies. André Gide's journals of the early 1940s record that Faulkner was a frequent subject of discussion among his literary friends. Still later, Albert Camus produced Faulkner's *Requiem for a Nun* for the stage in Paris. It might be said, parenthetically, that while Great Britain was not to share this French enthusiasm, there were a number of positive reviews of *Light in August*.

Faulkner's gradual rise to eminence in the United States can be attributed to several factors. First among these was his continuing publication of novels and short stories of very high quality. Another factor may have been the increasingly serious critical attention these works attracted. In 1939, George Marion O'Donnell published what would prove to be an influential and frequently reprinted essay, "Faulkner's Mythology."[4] He argued that Faulkner was a moralist with a strong historical bent, whose main subject was a socioeconomic and ethical Southern tradition in conflict with the forces of modernity. He described this conflict in terms of a basic Sartoris-Snopes opposition, and established its presence in a number of Faulkner's novels. He proposed a reading of *Sanctuary*—commonly considered a "potboiler" full of sex and violence—as an allegory of the rape of Southern womanhood by amoral Modernism. While O'Donnell's allegorical readings tend somewhat to rigidity or narrowness, it is clear that he recognized an underlying thematic principle in Faulkner's work, which many later critics would acknowledge.

Foremost among such later critics was Malcolm Cowley, whose Viking *Portable Faulkner*[5] was more widely accessible than O'Donnell's essay. Cowley wrote an introduction concerning Faulkner's creation of the mythical kingdom of Yoknapatawpha, which he compared in design and scope with Balzac's *Comedie Humaine*. Cowley arranged the stories and novel excerpts in this volume as a chronology of Yoknapatawpha from its earliest days to the present. Faulkner was now seen not only as the author of a number of distinguished individual novels and stories, but as a writer of grand design and near-epic scope.

Critical Reception

Faulkner's publication of *Intruder in the Dust* in 1948 sold extremely well, although it is by no means one of his best works. Some of its appeal may have stemmed from Faulkner's growing reputation, but a good deal of it had to do with the burgeoning civil rights movement and recent Supreme Court rulings against discrimination in housing on the basis of color or race. In the following years Faulkner would write a fair amount of nonfiction on racial problems in the South.

A Nobel Prize for Literature award in 1950 brought Faulkner increased attention. The book-buying public was now eager to read his work, and courses in American Literature in the universities were revised to give his writing more academic significance.

Even during the earlier years, Faulkner did not lack for appreciative reviewers and critics. *The Sound and the Fury* (1929) had been praised in a number of New York papers, including *World, Herald Tribune,* and *New York Times,* as well as in the influential *Saturday Review of Literature.* But, as Joseph Blotner points out, the Great Depression had caused a slump in book sales, which might in part account for the fact that despite strong reviews the novel's press run of only 1,789 copies was not sold out for a year and a half.[6]

The early reviews of *Light in August* were numerous and in-depth, suggesting that Faulkner's work commanded attention, if not always approval. There was a consensus that Faulkner's subjects were too depressing, morbid, or violent. As with any innovation in the arts, Faulkner's craft was not always appreciated, and his style and technique were felt by many to be obscure, or unnecessarily complex. These sentiments were by no means unanimous, however, and the novel was also praised for its intensity, its capacity for emotional involvement, and its style.

J. Donald Adams, a fairly conservative and influential critic, wrote in the *New York Times Book Review* (9 October 1932) that Faulkner had "for the first time" discovered justice and compassion, and praised him as a stylist. Another influential critic, Henry Seidel Canby, writing in the *Saturday Review of Literature* (8 October 1932), also praised Faulkner for his compassion, and found the novel to be of extraordinary force and insight, despite what he thought to be its obscurity, turgidity, and sloppiness in writing. On the other hand, Dorothy Van Doren, writing in the *Nation* (26 October), thought that Faulkner was merely repeating himself. She did not like the world that Faulkner wrote about, and accused him of creating people who lived "almost entirely in the viscera". Similar sentiments were expressed by Louise Field in the *North American Review* (January 1933), who found Faulkner's "very hopelessness, this sense of ills," to be too common in modern literature. Granville Hicks, a neo-Marxist critic at the time, gave Faulkner short shrift, judging him to be a searcher-out of despair and suffering, in which he found no meaning. His characters, Hicks claimed, came out of a pathology textbook, and he concluded that Faulkner hated humanity.[7]

In England, the anonymous reviewer for the *Times Literary Supplement* (16 February 1933) judged the novel to be "a compound of horror, hatred, lust, brutality, and obsession," but conceded that *Light in August* nevertheless displayed life with a "thunderous threatening beauty." The English novelist L. A. G. Strong, writing in the *Spectator* (17 February 1934), thought the novel "a fine, significant and important piece of work," a story that "burns throughout with a fierce indignation against cruelty, stupidity, and prejudice." Faulkner was hailed as the "coming American writer" by the novelist Arnold Bennett. Another distinguished novelist, Richard Hughes, was instrumental in getting Chatto & Windus to publish Faulkner's work. Other reviewers such as Compton Mackenzie and F. R. Leavis were impatient with Faulkner's style and "excessive" experimentation as a modernist.

From the American South, reviews were mixed. In the Macon *Telegraph* (16 October 1932), in a review headed "Thwarted Souls," A. B. Bernd wrote: "Save for his insistence that all the world is not only abnormal, but even nauseating and detestable, Faulkner has a first-rate talent." Faulkner's hometown newspaper, the *Oxford Eagle* (20 October 1932), gave a summary of other selective reviews, and concluded that *Light in August* was the greatest of Faulkner's novels.

Among the earliest full-length studies, Irving Howe's *William Faulkner: A Critical Study*[8] found *Light in August* especially significant. He claimed that Faulkner had moved from a rather paternalistic treatment of blacks, mainly as seen by white society, to a recognition in this work of blacks as distinct persons who are victims of injustice, kept on the margin of society, and therefore essentially homeless. At the same time, Howe expressed reservations about the form of the novel, which he thought had a "certain structural incoherence" (209), and about how seriously we are to take Lena Grove as anything but a simple country girl with a "vegetable-like" imperviousness to the complexities and miseries around her. He thought, too, that the unconvincing characterization of Hightower was perhaps "too close" to the author, serving merely as a mouthpiece for some of Faulkner's own nostalgia for an imaginary past.

Since the 1950s, *Light in August* has generally been accepted as one of Faulkner's best novels. It was published in that remarkably fertile period of some four years, 1929–1932, which also saw the publication of *Sartoris, The Sound and the Fury, As I Lay Dying, Sanctuary,* and the short stories of *These Thirteen.* Later critics have gone on to shed new light on Faulkner's sources and influences, his methods of writing and revision, and to offer new modes of interpreting the novel. Much good work has been done on Faulkner's themes— social, religious, historical—and on his techniques.

An interesting essay collection, *Religious Perspectives in Faulkner's Fiction* (ed. J. R. Barth, 1972), takes up a number of religious themes and issues, and raises the question of whether Faulkner's characters may be said to have real freedom of choice—a question that other critics have come back to frequently. A more general and intensive study of *Light in August,* by the French critic Francois Pitavy (originally published in France in 1970) was translated in 1972 (Indiana University Press). The author examines the background and composition of the novel, its structure and technique, style and themes, and critical reception. Pitavy also edited *William Faulkner's "Light in August": A Critical Casebook* (1982), which contains some very interesting essays on Faulkner's language and style, and on themes of identity and race. For more insight on the issue of race and its treatment, there is a very good study by Thadious M. Davis, *Faulkner's Negro: Art and the Southern Context* (1982).

Different critical theories and methodologies have been applied to the novel in recent years. Lee Clinton Jenkins published a study, *Faulkner and Black-White Relations: A Psychoanalytical Approach* (1981). In the same year Andrew Bleikasten's "Fathers in Faulkner" appeared in *The Fictional Father: Lacanian Readings of the Text* (ed. R. C. Davis, University of Massachussets Press). Structuralism is the topic of John Tucker in "William Faulkner's *Light in August*: Toward a Structuralist Reading," *Modern Language Quarterly* 43 (June 1982). The claim that Faulkner was a misogynist was advanced with some vigor by Albert J. Guerard in *The Triumph of the Novel: Dickens, Dostoevsky, Faulkner* (1976). A more balanced study, David Williams's *Faulkner's Women: The Myth and the Muse*, appeared in 1977. There is a sympathetic feminist study by Judith Bryant Wittenberg, "The Women of *Light in August*," in a very useful recent collection, *New Essays on Light in August* (1987), edited by Michael Millgate.

There is now an enormous body of criticism concerned with Faulkner's fiction, which includes the work of many of our most distinguished literary critics, and of academic studies and graduate theses. But no body of work has developed to challenge the high reputation of *Light in August* in relationship to Faulkner's other novels, or, for that matter, to the major novels of our time.

A Reading

4

Toward an Approach

Faulkner's reputation as a major novelist is secure. His work is completed, the evidence is in. He has provided several generations of readers with great pleasure and powerful imaginative experience. He created an entire fictional world in his Yoknapatawpha County, intense and vivid both as legend and as reality. His very best novels, *The Sound and the Fury, As I Lay Dying, Light in August, Absalom, Absalom!, The Hamlet,* and *Go Down, Moses,* as well as numerous short stories, place him indisputably among the greatest American writers. The challenge now for the reader and critic is to examine his values. What has Faulkner to tell us about our shared life, the confusing life of twentieth-century men and women? Does Faulkner, in an age beset by ideologies, have a consistent attitude and set of beliefs?

Some critics have suggested Faulkner is a pessimist who hates women (and perhaps blacks, too). Others have said Faulkner is a disciple of Rousseau, one who believes in the natural goodness of man and the social origins of evil, that he admires most the peasantry, or the noble savage, or the hill-folk of the South who speak simply but act grandly. He has been thought a romantic idealist, an exponent of the Good Old Days, with white mansions occupied by gallant and chivalrous gentlemen and their beautiful and (mainly) virtuous wives, around whom the Darkies spend most of their time singing spirituals with childish loving trust. All of this is thought to be depicted in a sharp contrast to the modern age, with its apparent lack of honor, chivalry, and gracious living.

Faulkner has been defined as a determinist who denies to human beings the exercise of free will, the ability to choose or to govern their own lives. The famous French novelist André Gide once wrote that Faulkner's characters have no souls, by which I believe he meant that they seem deprived of any spiritual autonomy in living out their destinies.

All of these categories are unsatisfactory. They contain elements that appear to be true, or are only sometimes true, together with elements that are overly simplified, or false.

Finally, in this brief review, there is the Faulkner who might be defined as a religious, even a Christian novelist. The strongest and most explicit case for seeing him this way was made by Randall Stewart in *American Literature and Christian Doctrine*: "Faulkner embodies and dramatizes the basic Christian concepts so effectively that he can with justice be regarded as one of the most profoundly Christian writers in our time. There is everywhere in his writings the basic premise of Original Sin; everywhere the conflict between the flesh and the spirit. One finds also the necessity of discipline, of trial by fire in the furnace of affliction, of sacrifice and the sacrificial death, of redemption through sacrifice. Man in Faulkner is a heroic, tragic figure."[1]

Much that Stewart says is true, or at least partially true; but he has laid claim too sweepingly to many qualities which one finds in pre-Christian, and non-Christian, literature. The Greek tragedians also said moving things about the conflicts of the flesh and the spirit, and of redemption through sacrifice, and Stewart leaves out Faulkner's silence or ambiguity on several aspects of Christian doctrine that I think are quite important. The concept of grace is one, a belief in God is another. But Stewart points to what I take to be central to Faulkner's fiction. While the degree to which Faulkner may be characterized as a

24

specifically Christian novelist remains debatable, Faulkner is a religious writer in that he is a writer concerned with searching for the values that govern and give meaning to human life, and with the nature and power of good and evil. My reading of *Light in August* is based on this assumption, although it will consider some other issues as well. I propose to consider only Faulkner's fiction, rather than what his beliefs might have been. Faulkner made a number of statements about his beliefs and his religious values, especially in his later years. These are often interesting, but they are not always the same beliefs one finds in his fiction.

5

In Search of a Theme

Light in August contains a number of stories, the most sustained of which is about Joe Christmas. But the novel opens with a long description of the pilgrimage of Lena Grove. While she rests along a country road, the author gives us a compressed history of her life and the circumstances that have brought her to where we find her. She is country-bred, an orphan, unmarried, and pregnant. With great innocence, and great faith, she has set out to find one Lucas Burch, the father of her unborn child, who had promised to send for her so that they could get married. Faulkner does not tell us that Lucas Burch probably has no such intention; nor does he tell us that Lena Grove is simple, naive, and trusting. Instead, he creates character through his narrative style, which has the flavor and the cadences of folktale and country talk.

> "How far you going?" he says.
> "I was trying to get up the road a pieceways before dark," she says. She rises and takes up the shoes. She climbs slowly and deliberately into the road, approaching the wagon. Armstid does not descend to help her. He merely holds the team still while she

climbs heavily over the wheel and sets the shoes beneath the seat. Then the wagon moves on. "I thank you," she says. "It was right tiring afoot."

Apparently Armstid has never once looked full at her. Yet he has already seen that she wears no wedding ring. He does not look at her now. Again the wagon settles into its slow clatter. "How far you come from?" he says.

She expels her breath. It is not a sigh so much as a peaceful expiration, as though of peaceful astonishment. "A right good piece, it seems now. I come from Alabama."[2]

The writing is slow, earthy, deliberate, even a little solemn, but with occasional flashes of laconic humor: "She had lived there eight years before she opened the window for the first time. She had not opened it a dozen times hardly before she discovered that she should not have opened it at all. She said to herself, 'That's just my luck' " (p. 3).

•   •   •

In his later years, William Faulkner claimed that his original idea for *Light in August* was the figure of Lena Grove, "a young girl with nothing, pregnant, determined to find her sweetheart."[3] At some point in the writing process he added another story involving Reverend Gail Hightower; or possibly Hightower was only intended to be the reflective center of the narrative. The Hightower story gave rise to the provisional title Faulkner assigned to his work in progress, *Dark House*. Only later, apparently, did he decide to have the figure of Joe Christmas dominate the novel.[4] In the completed work each of these characters generates his or her own narrative center, each with its own dramatic situation, attendant characters, and past history. And each has its own conclusion.

Lena's journey unfolds in a prose rhythm marked frequently by the repetition of such words as "serene," "peace," and "tranquil," which help to create the mild, trusting, accepting quality of Lena Grove. She has traveled mainly by foot for a long while.

Faulkner's description of her journey, although not in her own language, seems very close to her own consciousness: "Behind her the four weeks, the evocation of *far*, is a peaceful corridor, paved with unflagging and tranquil faith and peopled with kind and nameless faces and voices" (4). "How far you come from?" Armstid asks as they ride along in his wagon: "She expels her breath. It is not a sigh so much as a peaceful expiration, as though of peaceful astonishment. 'A right good piece, it seems now. I come from Alabama' " (p. 9).

At the same time, some descriptions of place are clearly separate from Lena's consciousness; they are unexpectedly eloquent, and highly rhetorical: "But some of the machinery would be left . . . gaunt, staring, motionless wheels rising from mounds of brick rubble and ragged weeds with a quality profoundly astonishing, and gutted boilers lifting their rusting and unsmoking stacks with an air stubborn, baffled and bemused" (2). Here is one of Faulkner's favorite stylistic devices—the use of three adjectives in surprising conjunction. The unexpected alternation of folk rhythms—which seem to come directly from Lena's world—with a high rhetoric—which seems to come from the author brooding on the scene—is remarkable. It conveys to the reader the felt lives of Lena Grove and the country people she encounters along her way. At the same time, it places us above this world, with a sense of epic timelessness, "like something moving forever and without progress across an urn" (5). Lena is a simple country girl, yet many readers and critics see her as emblematic of the life of nature, or as a kind of earth mother.

What is especially distinctive in the opening chapter is the impression of slowness and stillness. Lena walks about a mile, and up a hill; after having seen a wagon standing beside the road, she then waits for it: "The sharp and brittle crack and clatter of its weathered and ungreased wood and metal is slow and terrific: a series of dry sluggish reports carrying for a half mile across the hot still pinewiney silence of the August afternoon. Though the mules plod in a steady and unflagging hypnosis, the vehicle does not seem to progress. It seems to hang suspended in the middle distance forever and forever, so infinitesmal is its progress, like a shabby bead upon the mild red string of road" (5–6).

Shortly after this description the narrative perspective shifts, and we see Lena as she is viewed by the two men at the wagon: "The woman went on. She had not looked back. She went out of sight up the road: swollen, slow, deliberate, unhurried and tireless as augmenting afternoon itself. She walked out of their talking too; perhaps out of their minds too" (7).

Then Armstid, having concluded his business, drives his wagon along the road toward the top of the hill: "In the instant in which he recognizes the blue dress he cannot tell if she has ever seen the wagon at all. And no one could have known that he had ever looked at her either as, without any semblance of progress in either of them, they draw slowly together as the wagon crawls terrifically toward her in its slow palpable aura of somnolence and red dust in which the steady feet of the mules move dreamlike" (8).

In the conversations between Armstid and Lena, and later those involving Mrs. Armstid, we are struck by the careful and closely recorded speech of these country people, governed by a code of manners as distinctive and well defined as the more frequently depicted codes of the Southern gentry. The speech of Lena and the Armstids is slow, deliberate, diffident and marked by a native courtesy and careful observance of good manners: "She looks up at the sun. 'I reckon it's time to eat,' she says. He watches from the corner of his eye as she opens the cheese and crackers and the sardines and offers them. 'I wouldn't care for none,' he says. 'I'd take it kind for you to share.' 'I wouldn't care to. You go ahead and eat.' "(25).

Everything here is unhurried, peaceful, civil, and timeless.

• • •

The first several chapters of *Light in August* involve us totally with the journey of Lena Grove and her quest for the father of her unborn child. Chapter two introduces us to Byron Bunch, another country-bred figure, who works in the Jefferson mill, through whose eyes we first meet Joe Christmas (three years before the present action of the novel). Byron's impressions are definite and precise, and perhaps almost *too* perceptive, given what Faulkner tells us about Byron's sheltered life. This initial glimpse of Joe Christmas registers what will prove to be most significant about him, literally and symbolically, in the developing narrative. Byron notes Joe's arrogance, ruthlessness, and pride, as well as his rootlessness, homelessness, and loneliness. He is a marked man, suggesting the qualities of both ruthless aggressor and hopeless victim: "he wore a tie and a stiffbrim straw hat that was quite new, cocked at an angle arrogant and baleful above his still face. He did not look like a professional hobo in his professional rags, but there was something definitely rootless about him, as though no town nor city was his, no street, no walls, no square of earth his home. And that he carried his knowledge with him always as though it were a banner, with a quality ruthless, lonely, and almost proud" (27).

Now, moving forward again to the fictional present, Byron meets Lena Grove, newly arrived in Jefferson. For the first time in his life he falls in love, "contrary to all the tradition of his austere and jealous country raising" (44).

In Chapter 3, we are introduced to the figure of the isolated and shunned former minister, Gail Hightower, whose history during his seven years in Jefferson we are given, also partially, through the point of view of Byron Bunch. This technique of presentation helps sustain some sense of connection with the earlier narrative. When Byron comes to visit Hightower in Chapter 4, we learn through Byron's conversation that Joanna Burden, a white spinster, has been murdered, allegedly by Joe Christmas, who was her lover. Even worse, Christmas is now revealed to be a black man. It is difficult to conceive of a more incendiary situation in the American South of the 1930s.

In Chapter 5 we move abruptly again—now to Joe Christmas— during some 24 hours (as we only gradually discover) before this murder has taken place. It is, roughly, the same time period as Lena's chronicled travel toward Jefferson (although, again, we don't yet realize this). Here the writing is fairly objective. We enter very little into Joe's own point of view, thoughts or feelings. We are somewhat mystified about what is driving him, but it is clear that he is a driven man. There are unexplained allusions: " 'It's because she started praying over me,' he said . . . 'That's it. Because she started praying over me' "

(98). There are violent and sinister episodes. He manhandles Brown, who has returned to their cabin drunk: "He stood in the darkness above the prone body, with Brown's breath alternately hot and cold on his fingers, thinking quietly *Something is going to happen to me. I am going to do something*

Without removing his left hand from Brown's face he could reach with his right across to his cot, to his pillow beneath which lay his razor with its five inch blade. But he did not do it. Perhaps thinking had already gone far enough and dark enough to tell him *This is not the right one*" (97).

There are startling and violent images, without any explanatory context: "In the less than halflight he appeared to be watching his body, seeming to watch it turning slow and lascivious in a whispering of gutter filth like a drowned corpse in a thick black pool of more than water" (99). He drops his underwear—the only garment he is wearing—and exposes himself to the headlights of a passing car. Returning to his cabin, he is restless; he wraps himself in a cotton blanket and moves toward a stable: "It was falling down and there had not been a horse in it in thirty years, yet it was toward the stable that he went. He was walking quite fast. He was thinking now, aloud now, 'Why in hell do I want to smell horses?' Then he said, fumbling: 'It's because they are not women. Even a mare horse is a kind of man'" (101).

His actions, vividly described, are inexplicable, so that he affects the reader with the fascinating horror of a nightmare. The withholding of any explanation as to his background, his motivations, or his intentions, coupled with the lucidity and immediacy of description, is powerful, obsessive, even terrifying. Then, in a long circuit of seven chapters (6 through 12), we go backward in time for a very circumstantial history of Joe Christmas, before we are returned to the present again in Chapter 13.

These seven chapters—the longest uninterrupted narrative sequence in the novel—are also powerfully written. The author demands of us considerable identification with his main character, but provides a minimum of subjective characterization. We are close to Joe Christmas, but not often inside him. In these chapters, as in the earlier ones, the novel is presented primarily in dramatic scenes—as in a screen play—with a minimum of exposition or summary. Characteristically, the reader is pulled into a series of single episodes, between which there may be rapid background sketches—of earlier biography, for instance, or of summary narrative that may cover longer periods of time between the individual scenes. Henry James, in writing of the art of the novel, made a distinction between a "picture"—a summarized description or narration—and a "scene"—the dramatic representation of incidents and events. In *Light in August* it is clear that the preferred mode of fiction is the scene.

• • •

I have described the opening chapters not in order to give a plot summary of *Light in August*, but to convey a sense of the novel's remarkable range and diversity. Although all of the individual stories share a common space and time, they have little apparent dramatic unity. In terms of actual narrative plot, Lena Grove, Joe Christmas, and Gail Hightower are only marginally connected. Furthermore, Faulkner does not use the traditional devices of an omniscient author who brings his various characters and plots and subplots together by establishing some explicit framework of narrative or theme. Faulkner would appear to be less interested in a fictional structure that is organized through some traditional continuity of narrative, than in a structure dominated by the effects of juxtaposition—the placing of apparently unrelated scenes or episodes next to each other, with a minimum of transition or of connecting tissue between them, somewhat in the manner made famous by T. S. Eliot's *The Wasteland* (1922). The resulting sense of multiplicity, or even disjointedness, in the novel's structure has been ascribed by some readers and critics to Faulkner's weakness as a writer of novels (in contrast with his short stories), or to his obscurantism.

While it is true that the narrative structure of *Light in August* is loose, the novel is in fact integrated in a number of ways, the most important of which is the wide-ranging exploration of a dominating theme. This theme concerns the religious tradition of the American South and its grounding in Calvinism. The novel is concerned with two other themes as well, although these also have religious associations. One has to do with the relationships of blacks and whites. The other is the burden of the South's past and its traditions, so often seen as romantic, heroic, unfairly defeated, and tragic. But the single theme that serves most to unify the novel is that of Calvinism, and this I will discuss at some length.

The analysis of so inventive and complex an author as William Faulkner within so codified and consistent a doctrine as Calvinism inevitably confronts us with several inconsistencies and paradoxes. Not the least of these is that in *Light in August* Faulkner creates a Calvinist world in order to illustrate the negative effects of its doctrine on human relationships. At the same time the novel exhibits the continuous but unconscious influence of Calvinism on Faulkner's own attitudes, as a limiting frame to his vision, or as an emotional set.

Let it be said at once, Faulkner's concern with systematic religious doctrine is neither historical nor complete. Faulkner was not a theologian but a novelist. He did not write according to the original strict concepts of John Calvin or the historical Calvinist Church. The emphasis on the absolute sovereignty of God, for instance, with its hierarchal consequences in both Church and State, in no way concerned Faulkner, although strictly speaking this is the cornerstone of historical Calvinism. Calvinist Puritanism was one of the most important sources for the development of American civilization and culture. In the American North, Calvinism was particularly attached to the Presbyterian church, but this church was by no means the largest or most important in Southern life. However, in the South, most Protestant religions were strongly imbued with Calvinism: "... a Calvinistic tinge is apt to infuse the utterances of such non-Calvinists, strictly speaking, as the Baptists and the Methodists. The influence of Calvin is to be detected not so much in a literal application of the doctrine of the elect and damned, as in a serious and often gloomy view of man's fate, in an insistence upon strictness of behavior ... and in the belief, stated or implied, that sexuality is the chief sign of man's fallen nature."[5]

The Calvinism Faulkner treats in this novel is the religious and cultural residue of Puritan doctrine filtered down through the nineteenth and twentieth centuries of the American South. It is this doctrine that he attacks in *Light in August*. It is not simply the theology of a particular religion, but rather a set of attitudes, beliefs, and cultural practices that have been inherited from earlier religious doctrine. In time, doctrine may be diffused, separated from its institutionalized base, and become a dominant element in the very atmosphere that conditions our responses, without benefit of conscious credo, like a citizen who yells, "I've got my rights!" to an overstepping policeman at a moment when he neither knows nor cares that ultimately his doctrine is that of John Locke. It is at this level that Faulkner studies the effects of Calvinism on human beings and their relationships. And it is at this level as well that Faulkner's own unconscious Calvinism survives his conscious rejection of its hold on the human imagination.

6

The Shaping of Joe Christmas

The Calvinism that shapes and conditions the world of *Light in August* has a number of attributes, which I summarize here:

1. The institutional belief that elevates righteousness above love in its conception of the Godhead, and therefore also of human lives; a greater emphasis on Old Testament conceptions of God as a stern giver of law, who upholds justice, demands obedience, and is vengeful against sinners. Less emphasis on the New Testament conception of a mediating Christ, who advocates compassion, forgiveness, and love.
2. A morality that is implacably stern and judgmental in the weighing and punishment of human sin.
3. The belief that depravity is the natural condition of man; that the curse of original sin, stemming from the fall of Adam and Eve, taints all human beings for all time.
4. The belief that human sexuality is the primary sign and substance of this depravity; that the fall of Adam and Eve was the result of disobedience, whose expression is human sexuality.
5. The fear or distrust of women, particularly as the vessels of temptation and sexuality.
6. The belief in a strong measure of fatalism or predestination in human affairs.

These are the beliefs and attitudes that strongly affect the life of Joe Christmas, the novel's chief protagonist.

The story of Joe Christmas's doom is set within a contrasting framework of pastoral simplicity and natural goodness in the story of Lena Grove, who has traveled penniless and on foot from Alabama to Mississippi in search of the father of the child she bears during her long and beautifully evoked pilgrimage. Placid, trusting, innocent, her transparent goodness protects her from harm as invincibly as her very trust removes her from the need for protection. In her story good begets good; in Joe's story evil generates evil. Her world and Christmas's world represent two extremes.

Joe Christmas had lived for his first five years as a white child in a white orphanage, where he had been abandoned one Christmas Eve. Two circumstances shaped his future even more than the orphanage itself (although it is worth remembering that Faulkner's most famous villain, Popeye, in *Sanctuary*, was reared in an orphanage, as was a later unsympathetic figure, General Gragnon of *A Fable*). One of these circumstances, which Joe does not understand, is the pathological hatred which the school dietician comes to feel for him. Joe has been going to her room every day to steal a taste of pink toothpaste, taking so little each time that the loss is never noticed. But one day he is forced to hide at the unexpected approach of footsteps. He sits on the closet floor, covered with the dietician's "soft womansmelling garments" (112) eating toothpaste, hardly aware of her assignation with a young intern on the other side of the closet curtain. Only this time, trapped as he is, he eats too much toothpaste and is sick. When the dietician discovers him, she is convinced that he intends to reveal her transgression. She cannot conceive that Joe has nothing to reveal, except for his own crime; that his silence under her questioning is not cunning, but fear; that he expects not the dollar bribe she gives him, but a whipping. He is profoundly shocked by the lack of punishment. This is the first dislocation in what is to be a long series for Joe: "He was still with astonishment, shock, outrage. Looking at the dollar, he seemed to see ranked tubes of toothpaste like corded wood, endless and terrifying; his whole being coiled in a rich and passionate revulsion. 'I don't want no more,' he said. 'I don't never want no more,' he thought" (117).

In *The Sound and the Fury*, Quentin Compson's father tells him, "A man is the sum of his misfortunes"—a phrase that will haunt Quentin all through the day at the end of which he will commit suicide. Similarly, Joe's first misfortune results from the child's miniature Calvinist world of strict rewards and punishments being tampered with: "It never occurred to her that he believed that he was the one who had been taken in sin and was being tortured with punishment deferred and that he was putting himself in her way in order to get it over with, get his whipping and strike the balance and write it off" (115).

Moreover, the dietician has been led to believe (although it is not clear how) that Joe is black, and now she taunts him with this. She even tries to get him evicted by telling the school matron that he is black.

Here a second circumstance comes into play. The janitor of the orphanage, a dirty, half-crazed old man, has all along had some special secret interest in Joe. We will discover, very much later, that he is Joe's grandfather. In the present, however, his involvement with Joe is mystifying. Faulkner often refuses to "go behind" his dramatic scenes, to be an author who gives privileged information that is not called forth within the scene. Here, as is so often the case when Faulkner appears to withhold information, the object is not to tease or trick the reader, but to preserve the dramatic integrity of each episode as it unfolds. No one at the orphanage knows the real relationship that exists between the janitor and Joe, and the reader is limited to the information that is dramatically present.

Whenever the children are playing outdoors, the old man appears, quietly but unfailingly, to watch Joe. The dietician has observed this, and she comes to the old man now. She receives not his aid, but his curse: "Womansinning and bitchery!" He is not surprised that Joe has found her out (although the dietician has not told the janitor anything about the intern): " 'I knowed he would be there to catch you when God's time came. I knowed. I know who set him there, a sign and a damnation for bitchery' " (119). The old man kidnaps Joe to prevent

his being placed in a black orphanage. Before long Joe is found, however, and returned. There is almost certainly some religious symbolism
here, which I will take up in a later chapter.

This episode in the orphanage establishes a cluster of three associated ideas or motifs that are of paramount importance throughout
the novel: sex, black blood, and female lawlessness. Faulkner has
introduced first, sex, which Joe experiences here as a "primal scene,"
and which the old janitor believes to be emblematic of natural depravity. This sexual scene becomes associated with the pink toothpaste and
Joe's violent nausea. The second motif is Joe's "black blood"—not
the fact of it, but the allegation, as a taunt or gibe. Heretofore, in the
economy of his five years of life, this has had no importance for Joe,
although some of the children sometimes confront him with the word
"nigger." Why they do is never explained; the janitor claims they
simply "know." But at this crisis, at the moment of his ambiguous
discovery of sex, the "nigger" claim looms large. " 'You little rat!' the
thin, furious voice [of the dietician] hissed: 'You little rat! Spying on
me! You little nigger bastard!' " (114). And her "wild and dishevelled
hair" will be worth remembering when we come to Joe's later relationship with Joanna Burden.

Together with the motifs of sex and black blood, a third element
enters here: the evasion, by women, of law. Instead of beating Joe, the
dietician tries to bribe him. Later, after he has been adopted by the
McEacherns, a childless and isolated Scottish farming couple—he a
strict and literal Calvinist; she a wan, ineffectual shadow in her husband's life—Joe will come to despise his foster mother for her vague
conspiratorial attempts at tenderness, at love, at some consolation for
both of them for what McEachern has made of her. We can see Joe
trying to come to terms with some clear-cut system by which he can
safely measure his relations with the world, accepting even McEachern's system of unrelenting punishment as something he can understand and conform to. Joe accepts the "law" even when McEachern
whips him unjustly, by any reasonable standard; Faulkner describes
this episode in imagery that suggests an acolyte learning to undergo
the suffering acceptance of a stringent religious order: "[The strap]
rose and fell, deliberate, numbered, with deliberate, flat reports. The

boy's body might have been wood or stone; a post or a tower upon which the sentient part of him mused like a hermit, contemplative and remote with ecstasy and selfcrucifixion" (150).

But at the same time, Mrs. McEachern will try to undercut the system, to establish a more personal and tender relationship. "He seemed to recognize McEachern without surprise, as if the whole situation were perfectly logical and reasonable and inescapable. Perhaps he was thinking then how he and the man could always count upon one another, depend upon one another; that it was the woman alone who was unpredictable" (149).

What Mrs. McEachern wants to do, in the timid, conspiratorial manner that is the only way open to her under the domination of her husband, is to substitute love in the place of law. McEachern's life is controlled by his total and unquestioning acceptance of abstract principles. But Mrs. McEachern sees, more immediately and urgently, particular human relationships, which impel her not to defy these principles—she is too subjugated to do that—but to work around them as best she can:

> The man, the hard, just, ruthless man, merely depended on him to act in a certain way and to receive the as certain reward or punishment, just as he could depend on the man to react in a certain way to his own certain doings and misdoings. It was the woman who, with a woman's affinity and instinct for secrecy, for casting a faint taint of evil about the most trivial and innocent actions. . . . It was she who trusted him, who insisted on trusting him as she insisted on his eating: by conspiracy, in secret, making a secret of the very fact which the act of trusting was supposed to exemplify. (157–58).

When the dietician had attempted to bribe Joe with a dollar, she was motivated simply by self-interest and fear. When Mrs. McEachern sneaks food to Joe and invites him to share in her conspiracy against McEachern's law, she is motivated by simple maternal love. But this distinction is not comprehensible to the child, who sees only the disruption of a clear ordering of relationships. It is this evasion by women of law that Joe distrusts and that, ultimately, will lead him to murder.

This significant pattern of connected motifs provides for a central and unifying theme. It is no new insight that *Light in August* is in some way "about" Calvinism; what needs to be demonstrated is the central importance of Calvinism in the development of a strong thematic unity in a novel that has sometimes been called brilliantly written but disjointed.

The only times in the novel that Joe's black blood becomes important are when sex is important too: first in the episode with the dietician; later when in early adolescence he has his first sexual encounter in a barn, where he thinks he smells "womanshenegro" (147), and then goes berserk. Later still, he has a first love affair with the waitress Bobbie Allen, who also works as a prostitute (although Joe, seventeen and country-bred, does not know this at the time). This affair leads to his being brutally beaten up because he has confided to Bobbie that he might have some black blood.

Still later, Joe will encounter Joanna Burden—spinster, virgin, Puritan—who will at first yield to Joe only after fighting, but then will pursue and almost corrupt him: "wild then, in the close, breathing halfdark without walls, with her wild hair, each strand of which would seem to come alive like octopus tentacles, and her wild hands and her breathing: 'Negro! Negro! Negro!' " (245).

But during the long harrowing years of McEachern's domination, the issue of Joe's blood does not enter. McEachern's concern is with rearing an orphan who must be taught to be hard-working, obedient, chaste, frugal, and religious. His foster parents accept Joe—in their own particular ways—simply in terms of how he acts and what he does; they do not know that he may be a black. Neither do the people of Jefferson know, until after the murder of Joanna Burden, Joe's white mistress.

This consistent association of Joe's black blood with issues of sexuality has a clear thematic significance. As in any Calvinistic universe, the world of *Light in August* is a world of black and white, a world in which natural depravity, original sin, tends inevitably, even exclusively, to mean sex. This leads me to a crucial thesis about the novel: The terms *black* and *white* here refer not only to race but to something within the individual, to the radical divisions of the Calvinist world. In this world human beings are seen as either totally "depraved," or as achieving virtue only through God's election. The symbolic equation of blackness with real evil, or total depravity, will be found in the work of a few earlier American writers—most notably that of Hawthorne and Melville, especially in the latter's distinguished short novel *Benito Cereno*. In that work, as in Faulkner's novel, the conception of original sin goes far beyond the ordinary connotations of human fallibility and potential sinfulness, to conform to the Calvinist insistence on absolute depravity. Like Melville's Babo, Joe comes to represent this Calvinist extreme. But it is an extreme that will be found rarely in American literature after Jonathan Edwards.

Joe Christmas's father may have been part black—we never know for sure. Joe's mother had claimed that her lover was a Mexican (353–54). Faulkner is careful to leave the facts uncertain. Joe himself is not sure. "I think I got some nigger in me . . . I don't know. I believe I have" (184). This is relatively early in his life; later he will insist on his blackness savagely, vindictively. His blackness is significant precisely because he believes in it. The black comes to symbolize original sin; his bastard birth, his propensity to evil. More than that: Black here is not a symbol for *part* of each individual, so much as it is a symbol for a view of the total individual. For in Calvinism, as distinct from the central Christian tradition, the human beast *is* black, incapable of any redemptive goodness through his own effort, but only by and through God's mercy in His predetermined elections.

Joe Christmas's identity—the sum of his misfortunes—stems not simply from his displacement in two sociologically ordered Southern worlds of race. It stems also from an old Manichaean conflict between potential good and evil. Joe's vision of himself is finally of evil only— of total depravity—and it hurls him to a damnation that he believes is inevitable. The possible good in Joe is called into question by men, and frustrated again and again, ironically enough, by women. If Joe figures as a kind of perverted Christ symbol, he is surely also an upside-down Adam. But this irony is Joe's. The reader sees that his frustration comes not from any objective truth in his vision of himself, but from the vision itself, and from his consequent rejection of women (except as sex objects) and the feminine principle that transcends law, as Lena Grove transcends it.

Lena Grove's presence in the novel establishes the black-white conflict not as an inner struggle of all human nature, but as a struggle between two conceptions of human possibility: the Calvinist viewpoint, which Joe's history imposes upon him, and another, the term for which is perhaps a little more evasive: Romantic, Rousseauistic, the belief in natural man and in his essential goodness. The latter concept is exemplified by Lena Grove and Byron Bunch. If Joe's vision of evil hurls him to a damnation that he believes is inevitable, it is balanced in the novel—contradicted as a *necessary* view of human nature—by the vision and experience of Lena Grove, whose innocent assumption of universal goodness carries her in an opposite direction from Joe's. It is worth noting that Lena Grove has also sinned sexually, and by Calvinist standards ought to be regarded as damned, not only by her society but by herself. But her transgression is seen as innocent and natural, and she maintains a serene acceptance of herself as well as of her world. Even the virtuous Byron Bunch, himself a preacher of the gospel, is able to overcome his traditional insistence on "physical inviolability"—that is, on virginity—and remain steadfast in his love for Lena.

Joe has been pushed all of his life toward the black side—toward the worldview that the Reverend Hightower sees the church as too often embodying, its steeples "empty, symbolical, bleak, sky-pointed not with ecstasy or passion, but in adjuration, threat, and doom" (461). Joe feels himself to have been committed to evil and to damnation. Still, when Joanna Burden proposes that they marry, at that juncture in their relationship when the first outrageous passion has passed, Joe thinks: "Why not? It would mean ease, security, for the rest of *your* life. *You* would never have to move again. And *you* might as well be married to her as this—" (250) [my italics].

The vigilant reader will at once feel the separateness of this possibility from Joe's whole life. Its alien quality is emphasized by the fact that this is the only time that he thinks of himself as another person, as *you* rather than as *I*. Marriage to Joanna can mean something more than ease and security. It can mean also an end to flight, to his rejection of the world. But in another moment he thinks: "No. If I give in now, I will deny all the thirty years that I have lived to make me what I chose to be" (250–51).

What he has chosen to be is in fact what he believes to be predetermined: to be black and to fly from it; to see the possibility of being white and to reject it. The paradox (familiar to Calvinists) of *choosing* what is already predestined is echoed not long after, when Joe is sitting outside, waiting for that hour when he knows he will go up to Joanna's room and murder her. Faulkner describes his state in a rather tricky way: "he was the volitionless servant of the fatality in which he believed that he did not believe" (244–45). He believes that this murder is a "fatality" because Joanna Burden has started to pray for him.

She is the granddaughter of a New England abolitionist named, with a kind of double emphasis, Calvin Burden—the first name presumably in honor of the theologian who saw human life as a burden. Calvin Burden is a man who delivers to his son what he remembers of his own father's sermons, "half of . . . bleak and bloodless logic . . . and half of immediate hellfire and tangible brimstone." He is a man who can tell his children, "I'll learn you to hate two things . . . or I'll frail the tar out of you. And those things are hell and slaveholders" (229). His comments on the sinfulness and waywardness of the world are even more sublimely ironic: "Let them all go to their own benighted hell. . . . But I'll beat the loving God into the four of you as long as I can raise my arm" (230). The parallel with McEachern is striking, even if McEachern never speaks of God as "loving."

Joanna's father had taken her to see the graves of her grandfather and half-brother, shot down by the zealous Colonel Sartoris (who appears prominently in other novels, and whose murder of the Burdens is dramatized in *The Unvanquished*). These graves had been hidden for fear that townspeople still inflamed by the passions of Reconstruction might "find them. Dig them up. Maybe butcher them" (235). Her father tells her: "Remember this. Your grandfather and brother are lying there, murdered not by one white man but by the curse which God put on a whole race before your grandfather or your brother or me or you were even thought of. A race doomed and cursed to be forever and ever a part of the white race's doom and curse for its sins. Remember that. His doom and his curse. Forever and ever" (239).

This conception of the black man as the white man's curse and cross appears elsewhere in Faulkner. Its important racial and sociological implications require a separate treatment, especially since generally in Faulkner's work the "curse" is seen not so much as the black man, but as slavery, which doomed not only blacks, but the entire South.

In the dramatic context of this novel, however, we understand that when Joanna takes Joe as her lover so furiously, she is embracing not merely an individual man, but the Fall. Her relationship with Joe is presented not as some ordinary "affair," or as an instance of casual sexual promiscuity, but as a violent descent into a sensual passion saturated with the sense of sin and damnation. Her passion is clearly identified with the idea of original sin—"the curse which God put on a whole race"—the blackness that is not racial, not a partial element of humanity, but the Calvinistic conception of man's total depravity.

•   •   •

Ultimately Joanna Burden comes to exemplify still another aspect of Calvinism. This is through her demonstration of the way in which sin can come to be welcomed, even celebrated, as the only medium through which some ultimate victory is possible—an extreme form of the familiar doctrine of the fortunate fall. Or perhaps sin is the only medium through which man can at last recognize his essential humanity, and so fulfill his destiny. When Quentin Compson insists that his sister Caddy has committed incest with him, it is because he wants to deny the stupid, meaningless promiscuity which her world can no longer recognize as evil, and which their father shrugs off as "a piece of natural human folly." Quentin prefers the "clean flame" of damnation to "the loud world." When Joanna Burden at last succumbs to Joe Christmas—to sex, or natural depravity—it is an inevitable if long-delayed collision with the very meaning of her life: "At first it shocked him: the abject fury of the New England glacier exposed to the fire of

the New England biblical hell. . . . she appeared to attempt to compen-
sate each night as if she believed that it would be the last night on
earth by damning herself forever to the hell of her forefathers, by living
not alone in sin but in filth" (244). We can no longer believe that either
is the victim of the other; they are victims together.

But for Joanna, the Puritan's inevitable passionate remorse follows the passionate sin. She turns from Joe as lover in order to reform
him, to establish him in the world. She even goes so far as to suggest
a new career that will allow him some improper financial gain: "Then
I will turn over all the business to you, all the money. All of it. So that
when you need money for yourself you could . . . you would know
how; lawyers know how to do it so that it. . . . You would be helping
them out of darkness and none could accuse you or blame you even
if they found out. . . . even if you did not replace . . . but you could
replace the money and none would ever know . . ." (261).

When these efforts fail, she begins to pray for him. Once more
we have the pattern of black blood, sex, and a woman tampering with
inevitable law. Unlike Joe, she cannot accept her total, final damnation.
Trapped, as he feels, by a woman who will neither let him go nor
accept him for what he is, for what he "chose to be" (251), Joe murders
her and flees—a sinister figure with a baleful glare on his face, the sum
of his misfortunes embodied in his very clothes, the habitual uniform
of white shirt and black pants that tell his story.

• • •

I think it is important to consider at this juncture the claim that Joe's
hatred of women is the result of "latent homosexuality," a claim made,
for instance, by Cleanth Brooks in his introduction to the aforemen-
tioned Modern Library College Edition of the novel (xiii). This attribu-
tion of latent homosexuality seems to me a serious mistake about Joe
Christmas, and about the novel's meaning. It is true that Joe is suspicious of, and even hostile to, the "feminine principle." But Faulkner
never even hints at the issue of sexual preference. Rather, the concept
of the feminine principle is associated with the world of love, rather

than law; of compassion, rather than justice or retribution; and of decent human feeling, rather than divine or human violence. It is Joe's social conditioning that creates this hostility, and not some innate sexual bias. Furthermore, nowhere in the novel do we see Joe attracted to other men, or involved in any "male-bonding" friendships which might even suggest the idea of latent homosexuality. Indeed, at one point Faulkner may have anticipated some such theory about Christmas, and seems to contradict it quite explicitly: "His own life, for all its anonymous promiscuity, had been conventional enough, as a life of healthy and normal sin usually is" (246). What Faulkner contrasts with Joe's "conventional enough" sexual past is simply the unexpected debauchery of his liaison with Joanna Burden.

7

The Dark House of Gail Hightower

The third major story in the novel is that of the Reverend Gail Hightower. Fresh from his seminary, he had come to Jefferson as a minister because of his grandfather's adventures here during the Civil War. Hightower was the only child of a Presbyterian minister who was already 50 years old when he was born, and a mother who had been an invalid for 20 years. His childhood had been a lonely one, and he developed a greater emotional attachment to the memory of his dead grandfather than to his physically present parents. He regarded them, together with the black servant who was his nanny, paradoxically as the "phantoms" in his life. His grandfather, known to Hightower only through the oral history of his childhood, became the emotional center of his life, a figure enshrined in all the romantic, heroic imagery of the doomed, chivalrous exploits of the Civil War: "With this phantom [his nanny] the child . . . talked about the ghost. They never tired: the child with rapt, wide, half dread and half delight, and the old woman with musing and savage sorrow and pride. . . . He found no terror in the knowledge that his grandfather . . . had killed men 'by the hundreds' as he was told and believed, or in the fact that the negro Pomp had been trying to kill a man when he died. No horror here because they were just ghosts, never seen in the flesh, heroic, simple, warm; while the father which he knew and feared was a phantom which would never die" (452).

The circumstances of his grandfather's death are not revealed until the latter part of the novel. He had been involved in a successful raid on Grant's stores in the town, and later in a daredevil looting expedition, when he was shot by a householder while stealing a chicken from a henhouse. Bizarre as this is, Hightower's life remains fixated on the image created for him in childhood by his nanny: the moment of apocalyptic glory when the horses' hooves come thundering down the street and the troops descend upon the town. If the exact circumstances of the grandfather's death are kept from the reader until almost the end, it is because Hightower himself manages until then to block them from his romantic vision.

So central is this vision for Hightower that it becomes inextricably part of his religion. His early sermons, before he is forced to resign his pulpit, are compounded of a violent mixture of Christian dogma and martial glory, "up there in the pulpit with his hands flying around him and the dogma he was supposed to preach all full of galloping cavalry and defeat and glory" (57).

Hightower shocks and confuses his congregation, and totally neglects his wife. He is a man possessed, not simply by religious ardor, but by a fevered commitment to values that are violent and apocalpytic: "Then Sunday he would be again in the pulpit, with his wild hands and his wild rapt eager voice in which like phantoms God and salvation and the galloping horses and his dead grandfather thundered" (60).

Neglected, his wife is driven first to sordid liaisons, and then to suicide, and Hightower is driven from his pulpit. These catastrophes seem to overwhelm him, but not altogether; he still retains his emotional connection with the galloping horses. He lives as an outcast in a Jefferson rooming house, surrounded by an extremity of dirt and disorder that is as symbolic as it is physical.

In time, Hightower becomes painfully aware of the distance between the Christian gospel of love and compassion and the stern Calvinist religion of his community, which he himself had not merely sustained, but made even more inhuman and violent. He listens to the music coming from a nearby church and thinks, "the music has still a quality stern and implacable, deliberate and without passion so much as immolation, pleading, asking, for not love, not life, forbidding it to others, demanding in sonorous tones death as though death were the boon. . . ." He thinks of his land, his people, his own history: "Pleasure, ecstasy, they cannot seem to bear; their escape from it is in violence, in drinking and fighting and praying; catastrophe too, the violence identical and apparently inescapable. *And so why should not their religion drive them to crucifixion of themselves and one another?*" (347).

Here we can see that Faulkner had anticipated the vision of Albert Camus's influential novel, *L'Etranger*. We see that Hightower, as much as Christmas (or Joanna Burden), is an outsider. They are all alienated from any community; they exist on the margins of their society. They have no relationship with a group, a workplace, a neighborhood; they have no family. One consequence is that there is a terrible disparity between their rich, complex, and tragic inner lives and their outer lives—the ways in which they appear to live in the eyes of the Jefferson community. In the case of Hightower, he is simply a dirty old man, tainted by some old scandal already largely forgotten, living alone and virtually ignored by his fellow men.

Late in the novel, Lena has given birth to her baby with the reluctant assistance of Hightower. This intensely human involvement has served perhaps to pull him back toward vital life. Joe has been caught and murdered, despite Hightower's futile attempt to save him. In a very moving episode in Chapter 20, which is the climax and conclusion of his story in the novel, Hightower comes to realize that he has forfeited his life, and—quite literally—that of his wife, because of his allegiance not only to a dream vision of the past (a theme common to a number of Faulkner's characters), but to a conception of religion that is violent, apocalyptic, and dead. Too late, he recognizes his own culpability: "that which is destroying the Church is not the outward groping of those within it nor the inward groping of those without, but the professionals who control it and who have removed the bells from its steeples. He seems to see them, endless, without order; empty, symbolical, bleak, skypointed not with ecstasy or passion but in adjuration, threat, and doom" (461).

He remembers that earlier in his life, when he had first thought of a vocation in the church, he had believed in it, and had seen his future "complete and inviolable, like a classic and serene vase" (453). This image, which invokes Keats's Grecian urn, here suggests more than anything else an escape from the world and from life. It is paradoxical that he succeeds in retreating from all of the vital personal relationships in his life, while at the same time his religious vocation becomes hysterically alive with the imagery of death.

In the end he comes to realize that his great sin has been the rejection of his wife, who had offered him love. Only late in his life does he allow himself to recall their courtship and his binding of himself to her: "*The* woman. Woman (not the seminary, as he had once believed): the Passive and Anonymous whom God had created to be not alone the recipient and receptacle of the seed of his body but of his spirit too, which is truth or as near truth as he dare approach" (441–42).

But Hightower has wedded himself to his murderous vision of violent glory, like the Old Testament Apocryphal wars in heaven and on earth, and has dismissed his wife:

> I brought with me one trust, perhaps the first trust of man, which I had accepted of my own will before God; I considered that promise and trust of so little worth that I did not know that I had even accepted it. And if that was all I did for her, what could I have expected save disgrace and despair and the face of God turned away in very shame? Perhaps in the moment when I revealed to her not only the depth of my hunger but the fact that never and never would she have any part in the assuaging of it; perhaps at that moment I became her seducer and her murderer, author and instrument of her shame and death. (462)

There is clearly a parallel in the lives of Hightower and Christmas. Both have failed to form any vital human relationship; both have consistently rejected love from women. Christmas, in rejecting love, has taken only violent sex, recognizing only this as his human need and damnation. His repression of love leads to his intense loneliness, and ultimately to murder. Hightower, in rejecting love, becomes an outcast, known to no one except the kindly, sympathetic Byron Bunch. Too late, he comes to recognize that his wife's suicide was in fact his own murder of her, less flamboyantly violent than Joe's murder of Joanna, but equally heinous. And this murder is a miniature replica of his murder of his religion, to which he has brought "instead of the crucified shape of pity and love, a swaggering and unchastened bravo killed with a shotgun in a peaceful henhouse, in a temporary hiatus of his own avocation of killing" (462).

These recognitions do not come easily to Hightower; they are unspeakably painful, and he fights against them. But he is overwhelmed by memory, by the truth of memory, which Faulkner conveys dramatically in the image of a wheel mired in sand but slowly, relentlessly freeing itself and moving with its own inexorability: "Out of the instant the sand-clutched wheel of thinking turns on with the slow implacability of a mediaeval torture instrument, beneath the wrenched and broken sockets of his spirit, his life: 'Then, if this is so, if I am the instrument of her despair and death, then I am in turn instrument of someone outside myself'" (465).

A moment later, the rushing wheel seems surrounded by a halo, full of faces—the faces of his own past. Only one is not clear, that of "the man called Christmas" (465). This face seems a composite of two; then he recognizes the other face as that of Percy Grimm, the slayer and mutilater of Joe Christmas. Each opposes the other, yet blend, both as exemplars and victims of the ferocious religious compulsions that have shaped their lives—and his own.

8

The Avenging Angel

Still one other figure is important in this examination of the novel's themes: Percy Grimm, the man who shoots and castrates Joe Christmas. Faulkner would later describe him in a letter as a kind of proto-fascist, whom he had conceived two years before Hitler's ascendancy.[6] Grimm *is* a proto-fascist in a sense; but he belongs more immediately to a particular native American tradition of vigilantes, lynchers, and the Ku Klux Klan.

Faulkner's characterization of Grimm begins low-keyed, with a deceptive tone of sympathy. Percy is 25, and a captain in the state National Guard. He feels keen resentment at having missed World War I. His father thinks him to be rather worthless, since apparently he sees no challenge in the civilian life of a small Mississippi town. Grimm nurtures a private sense of tragedy because he was born too late. As compensation he is able to develop a belligerent patriotism, in which he finds his true vocation, as in a not altogether unrelated way Hightower had found his. "Then suddenly his life opened definite and clear. The wasted years in which he had shown no ability in school, in which he had been known as lazy, recalcitrant, without ambition, were behind him, forgotten" (426).

He becomes a "perfect" soldier, "completely freed now of ever again having to think or decide" (426). He is able to live happily with his "sublime and implicit faith in physical courage and blind obedience" (426).

This brief biography of Grimm, which has been presented with only the lightest touch of irony, sketches him with wonderful precision. But the characterization begins to darken considerably once Joe Christmas is returned from Mottstown to Jefferson as a prisoner. Grimm seems to recognize that he now has a special destiny, noble in his view for the opposition of his superiors to his excessively militaristic preparations. Once Christmas has broken free of his captors and is in flight, Grimm becomes another of the novel's undeviating champions of relentless justice; another pursuer, like McEachern and Hines. Now his characterization takes us back to the Calvinist Old Testament note of righteousness and violence, of judgment and doom. The seeds of Calvinism have flowered into public life, so that Percy Grimm is not a departure from, but an extension of the Calvinistic pattern of *Light in August*. His pursuit of Joe Christmas associates Grimm with the echoing tone of some infallible, inflexible Jehovah, relentlessly pursuing the enemy of law.

In the midst of Grimm's pursuit of Christmas we are given this startling image: "Above the blunt, cold rake of the automatic his face had that serene, unearthly luminousness of angels in church windows" (437). Then we read this curious passage, not about Grimm himself, but about Joe Christmas and the mob that has followed him into Hightower's house, where Christmas has fled: "Their faces seemed to glare with bodiless suspension as though from haloes as they stooped and raised Hightower, his face bleeding, from the floor where Christmas, running up the hall, his raised and armed and manacled hands full of glare and glitter like lightning bolts, so that he resembled a vengeful and furious god pronouncing a doom, had struck him down" (438).

When Hightower attempts to stop Grimm with his feeble alibi that Christmas had been with him on the night of the murder, " 'Jesus Christ!' Grimm cried, his young voice clear and outraged like that of a young priest" (439). He flings Hightower aside and runs on: "It was as though he had been merely waiting for the Player to move him again, because with that unfailing certitude he ran straight to the kitchen and into the doorway, already firing, almost before he could have seen the table overturned and standing on its edge across the corner of the room, and the bright and glittering hands of the man who crouched behind it" (p. 439).

He castrates Joe Christmas, who is not yet dead; the image of the "young priest" is gruesomely extended in this perverted religious ritual as he cries out, "Now you'll let white women alone, even in hell."

Surely it is remarkable that a deadly manhunt for an escaped prisoner accused of murder should be accompanied by so much religious imagery. We seem to be translated from the domain of fictional realism to that of theological drama.

• • •

There is a fascinating similarity between Faulkner's conception of Percy Grimm and an earlier fictional character, another pursuer driven by extreme inner compulsions. This is the character of Javert, the relentless policeman of Victor Hugo's famous novel, *Les Miserables* (1862). It is difficult to establish whether Faulkner had read this novel when he wrote *Light in August*, although it is known that Faulkner as a young man had read some Hugo, in translation.[7]

In Hugo's novel Javert, after many years, has discovered the true identity of the novel's hero, Jean Valjean, who had escaped after serving harsh years as a prisoner in the galleys for having stolen a loaf of bread. Hugo's understanding of Javert's feelings as he is about to apprehend Jean Valjean is curiously close to Faulkner's depiction of Percy Grimm, even down to a similar, if somewhat more romantic, use of religious imagery:

> Javert was at this moment in heaven. . . . he, Javert, personified justice, light, and truth, in their celestial function as destroyers of evil. He was surrounded and supported by infinite depths of authority, reason, precedent, legal conscience, the vengeance of the law,

all the stars in the firmament; he protected order, he hurled forth the thunder of the law, he avenged society, he lent aid to the absolute; he stood erect in a halo of glory; there was in his victory a reminder of defiance and of combat; standing haughty, resplendent, he displayed in full glory the superhuman beastliness of a ferocious archangel; the fearful shadow of the deed which he was accomplishing, made visible in his clenched fist, the uncertain flashes of the social sword; happy and indignant, he had set his heel on crime, vice, rebellion, perdition and hell, he was radiant, exterminating, smiling; there was an incontestable grandeur in this monstrous St. Michael.

Javert, though hideous, was not ignoble. The pitiless sincere joy of a fanatic in an act of atrocity preserves an indescribably mournful radiance, which inspires us with veneration. Without suspecting it, Javert, in his fear-inspiring happiness, was pitiable, like every ignorant man who wins a triumph. Nothing could be more painful and terrible than this face, which revealed what we may call all the evil of good.[8]

Like Percy Grimm, Javert has so internalized abstract conceptions of duty—as both a social and a religious concept—that he has lost all sense of, and all compassion for, human frailty, whether in himself or in others. For both Javert and Grimm, the commitment to vengeful justice is ruthless and impersonal, and they act as if with the firm conviction that they are the embodiment of higher laws, even perhaps of a higher Being.

• • •

It is a full gallery that Faulkner presents: There is Christmas himself, shaped by a Calvinist milieu and pursuing a Calvinist fate. There is McEachern, his Presbyterian foster father who has spent all one Sunday torturing Joe, self-righteously, because the boy has not learned his catechism. He beats and starves him almost to insensibility, then, late that night, he bids Joe to get out of bed and onto his knees to pray with him that God forgive the boy's evil. McEachern ends his prayer with the pious request that the "Almighty be as magnanimous as himself" (143).

Faulkner adds to these characters a number of others, perpetrators of every kind of violence, but who are themselves victims of a cultural obsession: Percy Grimm, Gail Hightower, and Joanna Burden. Joanna's whole life, of stoic self-denial and sexual repression, is challenged by the appearance of Joe Christmas. She flings herself into a life of desperate debauchery and sexual neurosis until she is overwhelmed by remorse and the urge to repentance. Then there is Eupheus Hines, the crazed white grandfather whom we meet early in the novel as the orphanage janitor, and who returns as the novel nears its end as a religious fanatic preaching a kind of pentecostal white supremacy in black churches. Hines calls himself an agent of God but (like McEachern) sometimes forgets that he is an agent only: "[he] was going singlehanded into remote negro churches and interrupting the service to enter the pulpit and in his harsh, dead voice and at times with violent obscenity, preach to them humility before all skins lighter than theirs, preaching the superiority of the white race. . . . Perhaps they took him to be God Himself, since God to them was a white man too and His doings also a little inexplicable" (325).

Later, Hines stands in the Jefferson streets screaming for the lynching of his grandson. He clearly is mad, but his moral exaltation has survived. It is clear that Hines suffers from a racial obsession as well as a religious one. But I am concerned with demonstrating that in this novel the two are inseparably linked by Calvinism. And it is this Calvinism, in its myriad forms, implications, and consequences, that the author so devastatingly indicts.

9

Faulkner's Own Dark House

Yet somehow a residue is left. There remains a sense of an underlying Calvinism that belongs to Faulkner himself, rather than to the condemned world of his characters. Against these characters, the story of Lena and her pilgrimage, her baby, and the attendant Byron Bunch should read like a final displacement of violence, an end to the resistance of evil with evil. It suggests the coming of Mary and Joseph and, perhaps, a loved and loving infant to take the place of the crucified Joe Christmas. But the balance of vision is not altogether convincing. It is as though Faulkner has come to reject Calvinism intellectually, even in some measure emotionally. But he has not been able, in Keats's fine phrase, to convince his nerves. What I have identified as a last residue of Calvinism, as a conditioning to vision and to emotional set—this endures in Faulkner.

It endures in one of Faulkner's characteristic styles, for instance: violent, tortured, doom-ridden, apocalyptic. Some years ago Warren Beck wrote a fine study on Faulkner's style. Some of his quoted illustrations seem to me especially interesting because they unintentionally reveal a Calvinist fixation on Faulkner's part, which is not the subject of Beck's article. Thus, when Beck comments on Faulkner's tendency to use repetition as a stylistic device, he cites these words as examples from *Absalom, Absalom!*: "effluvium, outrage, grim, indomitable, ruthless, fury, fatality—." He goes on to comment on Faulkner's occasional "prolixity," and gives this example from *The Wild Palms*: "It was the mausoleum of love, it was the stinking catafalque of the dead corpse borne between the olfactoryless walking shapes of the immortal unsentient demanding human meat."[9]

Faulkner's literal referent in this passage is not the Inferno, but the city of Chicago! Its tone of emotional rejection, of passionate revulsion, belongs to the Calvinist world of Jonathan Edwards.

Faulkner's own Calvinism endures, more curiously, in his treatment of time. I am convinced that it is just this note of fatality, of predetermination, that is responsible for the phenomenon that Jean-Paul Sartre, among others, has noted in Faulkner.[10] The impression he gives is of static time, of a present constantly exploding its connection with the past and disgorging not into the future, but into the moment that succeeds and is another *present*. Faulkner's time, to apply in a different way one of his own favorite images, is like a string of beads, each of which is the present moment as it meets the eye, and each alone. For in the Calvinistic conception of predestination, all time past and future lies in the present moment, caught suspended in the eternity of God's mind. Foreknowledge and predestination are equally divine attributes, and so all human experience becomes static in the fixed focus of the divine vision.

Thus, driven by some force outside himself, he waits during the hour before midnight for what he knows will be his final assignation with Joanna Burden. He thinks of himself as the "volitionless servant of the fatality in which he believed that he did not believe" (264). What Faulkner suggests in this passage—as compressed and knotted as a line of metaphysical poetry—is that Joe wishes to cling to the illusion of free will, of the ability to choose his own actions. But despite this illusion, he is driven by a fatality before which he is powerless. In the same passage, Faulkner stresses not only the note of fatalism, but the separation of this act from the normal (i.e., causal) flow of time: "He was saying to himself *I had to do it* already in the past tense: *I had to do it*" (264). This sense of fatality, or of predestination, is enhanced by the fact that the episode in which Joe awaits the hour of his last assignation with Joanna has already been described in Chapter 5, before we are given the long history of Joe's life that has brought him to the actual murder, in Chapter 12 (267).

The Calvinism of Faulkner is revealed in two other important ways in *Light in August*. The more immediately fascinating is the recurring theme of vengeful and fatalistic pursuit. The second, which I will discuss later, is Faulkner's almost universal association of sex and love with sin and destruction.

It is remarkable that there are three pursuits in the novel, all accomplished under astonishingly similar circumstances. The first (in order of the narrative sequence, rather than of the events themselves) is McEachern's pursuit of Joe Christmas, when McEachern discovers Joe sliding down a rope from his room. The foster father knows Joe is driven by lust. We are told that although he "had never committed lechery himself and . . . had not once failed to refuse to listen to anyone who talked about it" (188) and although Joe has never once even intimated that he has ever met a girl, McEachern nevertheless *knows*. He pursues Joe, who has long ago disappeared in Bobbie Allen's automobile: "He turned into the road at that slow and ponderous gallop, the two of them, man and beast, leaning a little stiffly forward . . . as if in that cold and implacable and undeviating conviction of both omnipotence and clairvoyance of which they both partook known destination and speed were not necessary. He rode at that same speed straight to the place which he sought and which he had found out of a whole night and almost half a county" (190).

Hearing music at a schoolhouse, he goes directly to it. He still does not know, in our ordinary sense, that Joe is there. When inside, his movement never once stops or is abated. He moves directly to Joe and accosts him. Like Eupheus Hines earlier at the orphanage, McEachern curses a woman, whom he regards as the vessel of sex and sin: "Away, Jezebel! . . . Away, harlot!" (191). At a high pitch of moral exaltation, McEachern feels himself to be the "actual representative of the wrathful and retributive Throne" (191). Joe strikes him and runs away; we never learn for certain whether McEachern has been killed.

The second pursuit is undertaken by Eupheus Hines, in search of his daughter and the circus man with whom he knows she is running away. Like McEachern, he does not know which way to follow. But he too sets off on horseback without question or hesitation:

> And yet it wasn't any possible way he could have known which road they had taken. But he did. He found them like he had known all the time just where they would be. . . . It was like he knew. It was pitch dark, and even when he caught up with a buggy, there wasn't any way he could have told it was the one he wanted. But he rode right up behind the buggy, the first buggy he had seen that night. He rode up on the right side of it and he leaned down, still in the pitch dark and without saying a word and without stopping his horse, and grabbed the man that might have been a stranger or a neighbor for all he could have known by sight or hearing . . . and shot him dead and brought the gal home behind him on the horse. He left the buggy and the man both there in the road. (355)

The sheer ruthlessness of this pursuit is not motivated by any desire to protect his daughter, as we will discover, but by an extreme vindictiveness in the name of righteousness.

The last pursuit is by Percy Grimm, who hunts down the escaped murderer Joe Christmas. Here, too, we have the same sense of fatality, of foreknowledge: "he seemed to be served by certitude, the blind and untroubled faith in the rightness and infallibility of his actions" (434). Faulkner evokes on at least three occasions the image of Grimm as functioning in "swift, blind obedience to whatever Player moved him on the Board" (437). Closing in on Joe Christmas with a terrible certainty of movement, Grimm moves with "the implacable undeviation of Juggernaut or Fate" (435) and "as though under the protection of a magic or a providence" (437). What must impress the reader in all of this is not that Grimm is convinced of his own infallibility, but that, in this event, he *is* in fact "infallible."

One such pursuit, so incredibly successful, might seem a coincidence; two, a cleverly calculated strategy of a very careful craftsman. But *three* so closely paralleled episodes—each involving an infallible pursuit, and each motivated by an inspired and vengeful judgment—surely suggest something more basic. That all three of these men believe themselves to be infallibly guided in the cause of righteousness is, of course, part of the very doctrine that Faulkner wants to reject. That all three should prove, in fact, to *be* infallibly guided—this is a fatalism that belongs no longer to the characters, but to the author himself.

I have emphasized the three major manifestations of this theme of foreknowledge, of mysterious "guidance." But these episodes, with their intimations of supernatural guidance, are supported by a number of other instances of a similar kind, less important in themselves, but contributing to a powerful cumulative effect. Joe for example, as a child at the orphanage scarcely knows the dietician, but "when he discovered the toothpaste in her room he had gone directly there, who had never heard of toothpaste either, as if he already knew that she would possess something of that nature and he would find it" (112).

Not long after the toothpaste episode, the dietician is visited by the janitor: "She did not, could not, know who it was, then somehow she did know, hearing the steady feet and then a knock on the door which already began to open before she could spring to it" (122). Later still, Joe goes to the place where Bobbie Allen lives: "The house was dark, but it was not asleep. He knew that, that beyond the dark shades of her room people were not asleep and that she was not there alone. How he knew it he could not have said" (186).

We have seen how McEachern pursues Joe to the country dance with absolute infallibility; but Joe too seems touched by a similar knowledge. He runs from the schoolhouse, having struck McEachern down: "He could not have known where McEachern had left the horse, nor for certain if it was even there. Yet he ran straight to it, with something of his adopted father's complete faith in an infallibility of events" (193–94).

Even Byron Bunch, who, like Lena Grove, seems quite unaffected by Calvinist doctrine, seems to be served by mysterious knowledge when he comes to rouse Hightower to assist with the birth of Lena's baby: "He had never been deeper into the house than the room where he had last seen the owner of it sprawled across the desk in the full downglare of the lamp. Yet he went almost as straight to the right door as if he knew, or could see, or were being led" (372).

Faulkner even gives us a comic variation on this theme in the utterly spineless Lucas Burch, in whom there is probably no more Calvinism than any other belief or principle besides that of seeking easy times and cheap pleasures. He is eager to claim the reward for identifying Joe as a black man who is the lover and murderer of Joanna Burden. But he is tricked into an unexpected confrontation with Lena and the baby that he has fathered. He flees in a craven way, and in a grotesquely comic sequence attempts to escape from Jefferson and, at the same time, collect his reward: "It seemed to him now that they were all just shapes like chessmen—the negro, the sheriff, the money, all—unpredictable and without reason moved here and there by an Opponent who could read his moves before he made them and who created spontaneous rules which he and not the Opponent, must follow" (414).

None of the instances I have cited need be considered especially significant; but together they contribute to the sense that Faulkner's characters are at least partly driven by powers of predestination or of foreknowledge. Later, Faulkner would insist on the reality of human freedom as a crucial part of human worth and dignity. But in *Light in August* the reader is almost overwhelmed by the sense that human fate is predestined, or totally conditioned, or controlled by the "Player" or "Opponent."

Only Lena Grove appears to move freely, without external manipulation. But there is a paradox even here. Lena is the only character in the novel whose movements appear to be fallible. She is given erroneous information on the whereabouts of Lucas Burch because her informants think she is seeking Byron *Bunch*. But in spite of this confusion, Burch proves to be where she seeks him. Moreover, she has her providential meeting with Byron Bunch as well. Not even the characters in the novels of Thomas Hardy are more governed by circumstance and fate.

Finally, what I have called the Calvinism of Faulkner himself is revealed in his fiction by the consistent association of sex and love with sin and destruction. It is curious that the criminality of Joe Christmas (as of the majority of Faulkner's most villainous characters) should be sexual, and that the motif of blackness, of depravity, should be worked out so exclusively in this novel in terms of sex. That sex is equated with natural depravity becomes even more clear near the end, when Grimm shoots Christmas and then castrates him. This emasculation takes on a grim symbolism when we realize that Joe's "black blood" can now, at last, leave his body. We are told that Joe, for the first time in his adult life not "baleful," not "sinister," looks through eyes that are *peaceful*. A moment later we are told that "from out the slashed garments about his hips and loins the pent black blood seemed to rush like a released breath" (440). On this "black blast" (440) the man soars into the memories of the Jefferson mob forever: "It will be there, musing, quiet, steadfast, not fading, and not particularly threatful, but of itself serene, of itself alone triumphant" (440).

That Joe, emasculated and dying, should invoke so startlingly the imagery of Keats's Grecian urn, is all the more startling when we remember that his first sexual experience with Bobbie is delayed by her being subject to that same periodic process that earlier in his life had caused Joe, learning of its existence, to shoot a sheep, and to kneel, "his hands in the yet warm blood of the dying beast, trembling, dry-mouthed, backglaring" (174). When Bobbie tells him that she is "sick," Joe strikes her and runs, entering the woods where, "as though in a cave he seemed to see a diminishing row of suavely shaped urns in moonlight, blanched. And not one was perfect. Each one was cracked and from each crack there issued something liquid, deathcolored, and foul. He touched a tree, leaning his propped arms against it, seeing the ranked and moonlit urns. He vomited" (177–78). We are taken back, of course, to the primal experience at the orphanage, when "ranked tubes of toothpaste" become confused with sex, and with physical revulsion.

I am tempted to remark, parenthetically, on the frequent and curious associations given to food in *Light in August*, associations most frequently unpleasant or foreboding. Besides this association of sex and the vomiting of toothpaste at the orphanage, we may remember that Mrs. McEachern's primary way of showing affection is to sneak food to Joe, which at least once he smashes against the wall, as he will do again in Joanna Burden's kitchen. He first meets Bobbie

Allen when he is given a dime and goes to a cafe to spend it on pie and coffee.

We may be reminded by the "urns in moonlight" passage quoted above of Keats's urn and of Faulkner's use of it later, as in *The Bear*, as a symbol of "honor and pride and pity and justice and courage and love," untainted by human appetites and greeds. But in this passage the allusion is ironically distorted. It is distorted again in the figure of Joe Christmas dying, creating an image "of itself serene, of itself alone triumphant" (440). It is difficult to imagine a stronger rejection of the entire human sexual process. The curse of original sin has been lifted; in mutilation lies our peace. What remains is serene and triumphant, purified and made white. The dying god, the maimed fisher-king, is translated to the heavens where no spring may touch him with renewal.

If we look elsewhere in Faulkner—as W. R. Moses has done[11]— we will find it hard, if not impossible, to find anywhere the theme of love or of sex treated as something positive in value, or involving the integrity of human choice. Love or sex will be seen either as an expression of a compulsive, involuntary curse or "possession," or as an expression of depravity or evil. Next to the fuller, more highly charged treatment of love and sex as seen from these perspectives, the pastoral story of Lena Grove and Byron Bunch, as beautifully as it is depicted for the most part, seems in the end something projected rather than achieved, something wished for rather than seen.

Their story has just begun at the end of *Light in August*, and even then it is reported only at secondhand by a furniture dealer invented for this brief occasion. This distancing of Lena's story at the novel's end has aroused some critical controversy, which I shall discuss later. Here I wish to point out that later in his career, Faulkner was never to take up again such a positive vision of love between man and woman.

Although not necessarily germane to a discussion of *Light in August*, it is interesting to note that with few exceptions, Faulkner's "admirable" women—the women, that is, whom he portrays in a positive light—are generally older, past the stage of sexuality and temptation that the Calvinist tradition associates with femininity.

These older women include Dilsey in *The Sound and the Fury* (who is also black, embodying very beautifully the qualities of love, compassion, and fidelity), Aunt Jenny in *Sartoris*, Granny Millard in *The Unvanquished*, and Miss Habersham in *Intruder in the Dust*. But Faulkner's fiction rarely goes beyond its distrust of women who are of an age to be still sexually active. A common charge against Faulkner is that he is fundamentally a misogynist. Such a view derives primarily from Faulkner's Calvinistic distrust of sexuality and its associations with sin. In *Light in August* Faulkner attributes to the dietician a "natural female infallibility for the spontaneous comprehension of evil" (117) in a way reminiscent of the long Puritan tradition of dealing with Eve in the Garden of Eden.

Lena Grove remains a singular exception to most of these generalizations. But it is striking that it takes the quixotically innocent Byron Bunch a terribly long time before the actual sexual facts of Lena's pregnancy and delivery register emotionally (379–80). He is able to accept these facts ultimately because he can transfer "blame" from Lena to Lucas Burch. His essential innocence is preserved in part through his chivalrous fight with Burch, who of course whips him thoroughly (415–16). His own courtship of Lena is reported indirectly, and without conclusion. The Lena Grove–Byron Bunch story is fairly consistent in its dealing with sexuality only obliquely and comically: It is Faulkner's version of Pastoral.

10

Religious Patterns

It is illuminating to consider briefly Faulkner's search for a coherent religious belief that might replace the Calvinism which, as we have seen, he both condemns and inadvertently reflects in *Light in August*. This search proved to be a tentative one. It took him to the affirmations of "The Bear" (1942), with its sacramental view of nature and its celebration of a wilderness which was already disappearing rapidly, but which might still give sustenance as an affirmative ideal in expiation for the social and sexual sins of the past. The protagonist, Ike McCaslin, renounces his family's land, which he feels is tainted by slavery and by the brutal miscegenation perpetrated by whites, and in a gesture suggestive of Christian symbolism, takes up the life of a carpenter. But despite his exemplary development in "The Bear," Ike is seen as curiously ineffectual in other stories in *Go Down, Moses*, the work in which "The Bear" appears. Faulkner holds Ike up for admiration at the same time that he must acknowledge the unlikelihood that he will serve as a model for the lives to which the twentieth century commits us.

Faulkner's spiritual search took him to *Requiem for a Nun* (1950), which is something of a sequel to *Sanctuary*. In the major section of this play, Faulkner wishes to affirm some kind of transcendental value through Nancy Mannigoe, a black woman who was once a whore and dope addict. She had appeared earlier in one of Faulkner's best short stories, "That Evening Sun," where she was working for the Compson family and undergoing suffering from which the Compsons were unable to offer any real help, but which perhaps brought her to her later faith. She remains less dramatically convincing than Dilsey, the previously mentioned black servant of the Compsons in *The Sound and the Fury*. Dilsey's love, devotion, and compassion are sustained by a clear religious faith that exposes the emptiness of the Compson values, and she is presented with less self-conscious thematic manipulation than is Nancy, and her faith, in *Requiem for a Nun*.

Nancy murders Temple Drake's baby in order to prevent Temple's debasement by way of a planned return to the sordid Memphis life of *Sanctuary*. Nancy, the "nun" of the title, is seen as motivated by a firm, if unspecified, faith that everyone in the novel comes to admire, as Faulkner himself clearly does. When the "spokesman" of the novel, Gavin Stevens, asks of Nancy her remedy for the violence and tragedy that so strongly color their world, her response is impressive; and yet, one must confess, it is vague in detail and possibly chilling in substance:

> *Nancy:* You don't even need hope. All you need, all you have to
> do, is just believe. So maybe—
> *Stevens:* Believe what?
> *Nancy:* Just believe.

What is affirmed, at the risk of sounding tautological, is faith in faith. I call this thematic development somewhat chilling because while faith may well be desirable, it must inevitably be grounded in some substance other than itself. One may have faith in God (or gods), in humanity, in science, in social evolution. Failing those, or other equivalents, faith seems as unavailable as the wilderness that Faulkner had celebrated earlier through his portrayal of Ike McCaslin.

Faulkner moves, finally, to the world of *A Fable*, which was published in 1955 (although he began work on it as early as 1944).

The "fable" is of a corporal who leads his twelve squad members, or disciples, in a pacifist movement during World War I, a campaign of nonresistance to evil that brings to mind the religious traditions of Tolstoy and Ghandi. The corporal is betrayed, judged, denied by a squad member named Piotr, and executed by order of the Marshal of France, who proves to be the corporal's "real" father. Before the corporal is executed, he is tempted by a general on a mountaintop with the lures of both worldly and spiritual power. Some time after his death, his body is returned to Paris as the result of some mysterious complications, and he becomes France's Unknown Soldier, thus achieving at least a nominal immortality.

Despite the religious paradigms, the novel's strongest single affirmation is in the belief that man will prevail, an affirmation that echoes very closely Faulkner's famous Nobel Prize acceptance speech of 1950. Admirable as it may be in conception, A Fable is a failure as a novel. It is Faulkner's most opaque book, the most tortuously written, the most dense in symbolism and in overly manipulated plot elements. It is as though his affirmations cannot be sustained through a more direct or more straightforward scrutiny. Even for a writer whose approach has always been somewhat oblique and complex, his procedure in A Fable results in an obscurantism that is far more significant than a mere failure of artistic control.

Two kinds of generalization may be drawn from the history of Faulkner's religious quest. The first is that in a general way Faulkner's fiction from roughly the 1940s on moves toward a more vigorous (and articulate) assertion of positive values; and his heroes or protagonists tend more to embody ethical commitments, or to be in search of transcendental values. The second, and related, generalization is that Faulkner apparently did struggle toward a faith, toward assent to some kind of transcendent religious value. This struggle, which was never altogether resolved, escapes any simple classification such as "Christian" or "Humanist," although it incorporates elements of both. What is significant is that this struggle may be seen as indicative of the intensely serious and ambitious scope of his novels and stories, unparalleled in twentieth-century American fiction. It is frequently the case that even Faulkner's weaknesses and failures are more rewarding than the successes—so small in comparison—of many modern novels.

This brief examination of religious symbolism takes us back full circle to *Light in August*. This novel, too, employs a good deal of religious symbolism quite aside from the explicit religious themes found in the story of Gail Hightower. It is a symbolism that defies simple interpretation. The novel's chief protagonist is left at a white orphanage on Christmas Day, and so is given the name of Joe Christmas, although perhaps with no more serious religious impulse than is to be found in our contemporary celebrations of this occasion. His life (and what Eupheus Hines thinks of as his "mission," to preserve Joe as a witness amongst the Philistines) seems threatened, and they escape the orphanage in a manner that may be symbolically parallel to the flight into Egypt of the infant Christ when threatened by Herod. Later, we will discover that Joe's paternity involves some mystery.

The details of his life as a young man are given in only a general way, and he reappears fully at the age of 33. The age of Christ at the time of his crucifixion and death is traditionally given as 33, and many critics have made the mistake of claiming this to be Joe's age at the time of his death. In the novel, however, it is clearly stated that Joe is 33 when he first appears in Jefferson as a stranger and begins working at the sawmill (213). We are told that he lives in Jefferson for three years (279 and 316), so that in fact he is 36 when he is murdered.[12] He is "tempted" with material and spiritual rewards by Joanna Burden, and refuses them. He murders Joanna on a Friday, and is captured (or may be) on the following Friday (but possibly on Saturday). He is betrayed by his disciple, Lucas Burch, for the sake of a cash reward. As an escaped fugitive, he is "denied" by Gail Hightower. He is mutilated and killed by a representative of the state, Percy Grimm of the National Guard. From the "black blast" of his death, there is an apotheosis, and at least a metaphoric immortality: "The man seemed to rise soaring into their memories forever and ever. . . . of itself alone serene, of itself alone triumphant."

Is Joe Christmas, then, a symbolic Jesus Christ? Such a parallel seems to me impossible to sustain, except in the very limited sense that

Christmas knows suffering and a terrible death. There is a similar symbolic parallel in the figure of Benjy, the idiot son of the Compsons in *The Sound and the Fury*, who suffers for the sins of his family, and is sent by his brother Jason to an institution to be emasculated. But the Christian symbolism associated with Benjy is equally incomplete, albeit tantalizing.

The religious symbolism attached to Joe is accompanied by a curiously related symbolism in the Lena Grove story. Lena—whose name suggests Mary Magdalen of the Gospels—bears a child. She is accompanied by Byron Bunch, who is not exactly a carpenter but works in a sawmill. There is no room for the pregnant Lena in Jefferson, and she must give birth to her child in the abandoned shack where Joe Christmas had been living. The infant is born early on a Monday, the same day that Joe Christmas is killed. Mrs. Hines confuses this birth with the terrible birth of her daughter's child many years before, and keeps calling Lena's newborn baby "Joey." This in turn confuses Lena, who says she sometimes thinks "that his pa is that Mr—Mr Christmas too—" (388). Here the metaphoric father and the son are given a loose kind of symbolic identity. And at the end of the novel we see Lena not fleeing danger, but resuming her "travels" attended by the saintly Byron Bunch, who is prepared to be the infant's adopted father: a holy family whose infant suggests a happier future than the perverted life and death of Joe Christmas.

What are we to make of these remarkable parallels? There is little warrant in assuming any literal or close connection between these figures and those of the central Christian story. It is more accurate, I believe, to say that Faulkner uses Christian symbolism as a culturally shared archetype in order to add resonance and universality to his story, especially in his concern for and use of the themes of human suffering and death. But the Christian symbolism is important also in relation to the theme of cyclical renewal, of rebirth and human continuity.

Indeed, such an interpretation is supported by Faulkner's comments to students in 1957. When he was asked about the recurring imagery of crucifixion in his fiction, he replied: "Remember, the writer must write out of his background. He must write out of what he knows, and the Christian legend is part of any Christian background, especially the background of a country boy, a Southern country boy. My life was passed, my childhood, in a very small Mississippi town, and that was part of my background. . . . It has nothing to do with how much of it I might believe or disbelieve—it's just there."[13]

11

Blacks and Whites

In the earlier drafts of *Light in August,* Faulkner identified Joe Christmas as a black man. But in his revisions he carefully removed these identifications, and left the issue of Joe's origins deliberately equivocal. Joe himself, as we have seen, says, "I may be [black]." The only character who seems certain that Joe is black is his grandfather, Euphues Hines; but since Hines is both a fanatic and at least half-crazed, it is not altogether clear that we should take his word for it. It is true that Lucas Burch, seeking the reward for the murderer of Joanna Burden, tells the sheriff that Joe is black. He has only a hint from Joe on which to base this charge, an allegation that stems in part from his own vindictiveness. Furthermore, he sees, quite correctly, that his disclosure is bound to inflame the townspeople and thus doubly assure Joe's capture and death.

A good part of Joe Christmas's tragedy is precisely that he himself does not know who he is. It is not merely an uncertainty about parentage, which might trouble any orphan; it is that his race, so crucial an issue in the American South, is ambiguous. Blacks in the South were assigned radically separate identities and expectations, and radically different relationships with whites and the dominant white culture.

Many years after the writing of *Light in August,* Faulkner told his audience at the University of Virginia that Joe's great tragedy was that "he did not know what he was, and so he was nothing. He deliberately evicted himself from the human race because he didn't know what he was. That was his tragedy, that to me was the tragic, central idea of the story—that he didn't know what he was, and there was no way possible in life for him to find out."[14]

An important question presents itself: What is the significant interpretation we are to make of Joe as a black man? The answer must involve some consideration of Faulkner's known treatment of blacks in his fiction. Another question, which has really already been discussed, concerns the significance of the doubt about Joe's color that Faulkner presents.

We are never given a detailed description of Joe's appearance. We know that he frequently looks "baleful"; we know of his symbolically significant dress, a white shirt and dark pants. He is presumably of a complexion that allows him to be accepted as white, but that does not belie the allegations that he is at least part black. So far as his appearance goes, the suggestion, referred to earlier, that his father may have been Mexican is as reasonable as the supposition that he is (at least part) black.

In Faulkner's previously mentioned "Delta Autumn" (in *Go Down, Moses*), Ike McCaslin is visited by a young woman, the unmarried mother of his nephew's child. Her ambiguous appearance and status trouble him until certain signs push him to awareness: "Now he understood what it was she had brought into the tent with her, what old Isham had already told him by sending the youth to bring her in to him—the pale lips, the skin pallid and dead-looking yet not ill, the dark and tragic and foreknowing eyes. . . . He cried, not loud, in a voice of amazement, pity, and outrage: "You're a nigger!" At no point in *Light in August* does anyone "read" Joe's appearance in this way. But in a sense, his appearance hardly matters once the label "Negro" is attached to him.

It is easy enough to see that when Joe is thought to be black by those around him, any individual identity he may possess is eliminated and replaced by a stereotype—the stock response which "nigger" evokes. The fallacies about black behavior that had developed in the South are too numerous to catalog here; in addition to the stereotypical assumptions—of inferior intelligence, lack of motivation, brutishness or the absence of "fine" feelings—was the irrational fear that black males, especially, were animal-like in their sexuality, and, worse, desired above all else to cohabit with white women. These stereotypes exist as abstractions, without reference to individuals, or even to the personal experiences of the people who accept these abstractions as true.

After the dead body of Joanna Burden is discovered in the burning house, and Lucas Burch (under the alias of Joe Brown) has made his allegations against the lover-murderer of Joanna Burden, a lynch mob begins to form, "who believed aloud that it was an anonymous negro crime committed not by a negro but by Negro and who knew, believed, and hoped that she had been ravished too" (271–72).

That is why much later Percy Grimm, after he shoots Joe Christmas, stoops and, in a sadistic gesture—justified in his mind by righteous convictions about white retribution—castrates him and says, "Now you'll let white women alone, even in hell" (439).

It is obvious enough that Joe himself has suffered from much of this stereotyping. In addition, he suffers even when his being taken for black does not lead to the "proper" responses that his society has conditioned him to expect. Thus, for example, he beats up a prostitute after he has deliberately told her that he is black because she fails to become indignant, and instead is merely interested in receiving payment for her services. He deliberately taunts white men into calling him black in order to fight them, and then taunts blacks to call him white (211–12).

Several elements combine to make the novel's attitudes toward blacks difficult to draw out in an explicit way. Aside from Christmas, there are few blacks in the novel, and none is given a full characterization. The feelings and attitudes expressed in the novel are rarely those of the author, but rather the direct experiential feelings of the characters through whose points of view we experience the events. Among these characters—Lena Grove, Gail Hightower, Joe Christmas, and to a lesser extent Byron Bunch and Percy Grimm—only Joe Christmas has any major concern with what it really means to be a black man in the South.

In addition, the feelings of Joe Christmas himself about blacks are capable of being interpreted in quite different ways, especially if one makes the error of assuming that Joe's attitudes are the same as the author's. For instance, there is a striking passage in which Joe Christmas walks through Freedman Town, the black ghetto, shortly before the murder of Joanna Burden:

> Without his being aware the street had begun to slope and before he knew it he was in Freedman Town, surrounded by the summer smell and the summer voices of invisible negroes. They seemed to enclose him like bodiless voices murmuring, talking, laughing, in a language not his. As from the bottom of a thick black pit he saw himself enclosed by cabinshapes, vague, kerosinelit. . . . On all sides, even within him, the bodiless fecundmellow voices of negro women murmured. It was as though he and all other manshaped life about him had been returned to the lightless hot wet primogenitive Female. He began to run, glaring, his teeth glaring, his inbreath cold on his dry teeth and lips, toward the next street lamp. . . . panting, glaring, his heart thudding as if it could not or would not yet believe that the air now was the cold hard air of white people. (106–7)

• • •

In Myra Jehlen's *Class and Character in Faulkner's South* this passage is interpreted, plausibly but incorrectly, as an expression of Faulkner's own view that "black and white" are "physically rather than culturally distinct." Faulkner is said to assign a "sexual interpretation on each, which, as it were, piles sexism upon racism." This interpretation, that for Faulkner "racial character is a matter of physiology, and only secondarily psychological and cultural"[15] is supported, this critic believes, by an earlier episode in which Faulkner describes Joe Christmas's attempt to commit himself to a black identity by living as man and wife with a black woman:

At night he would lie in bed beside her, sleepless, beginning to breathe deep and hard. He would do it deliberately, feeling, even watching, his white chest arch deeper and deeper within his ribcage, trying to breathe into himself the dark odor, the dark and inscrutable thinking and being of Negroes, with each suspiration trying to expel from himself the white blood and the white thinking and being. And all the while his nostrils at the odor which he was trying to make his own would whiten and tauten, his whole being writhe and strain with physical outrage and spiritual denial. (212)

These responses of Joe Christmas must surely be seen as his own, the result of his traumatic associations of sex with sin and physical revulsion (as in the episodes of the toothpaste and the dietician; his adolescent initiation with the black girl in a barn; and Bobbie Allen). Because he has been reared in the South by whites, he has internalized white attitudes about blacks, and Calvinist associations of blackness with sexuality. But he is no more reconciled to the "cold hard air of white people" than to the "fecund" and "hotwet" and "Female" air of black people. To identify these responses with the views of the author is as mistaken as the identification of Gavin Stevens with William Faulkner, an issue that I shall come back to shortly.

Joe Christmas mirrors, in a grotesque and tragic way, the white ideas that have both shaped and condemned him. The possibility that Faulkner himself associates sexuality particularly with blacks is clearly contradicted, it seems to me, by his portrayal of Joanna Burden, a white woman who leads Joe Christmas into the wildest, and perhaps the most perverted, sexual encounters of his life. Indeed, Faulkner explicitly states that it is Joanna Burden who corrupts Joe at least as much as Joe may be seen as corrupting her: "The corruption came from a source even more inexplicable to him than to her. In fact, it was as though with the corruption which she seemed to gather from the air itself, she began to corrupt him. He began to be afraid. He could not have said of what. But he began to see himself as from a distance, like a man being sucked down into a bottomless morass" (246).

Expectations in the South about blacks' behavior were determined by generations of cultural conditioning, prejudice, and fear. Earlier, the morality of owning slaves had been upheld not only by the state but by the church, in part by some curious interpretations of the Bible to demonstrate the inferiority of blacks, who, it was alleged, were the sons of Ham, cursed by Noah. Although slavery ended with the Civil War, many of the earlier attitudes toward blacks remained, with only rare opposition from church or state.

When Joanna Burden tells Joe about her family's history, and her father's telling her of the white man's "curse"—the blacks—she recalls: "I seemed to see them . . . not as people, but as a thing, a shadow in which I lived, we lived, all white people, all other people. . . . And I seemed to see the black shadow in the shape of a cross. And it seemed like the white babies were struggling, even before they drew breath, to escape from the shadow" (239).

When she tried to tell her father that she must escape this burden, he insisted that she could not escape: "The curse of the black race is God's curse. But the curse of the white race is the black man who will be forever God's chosen own because He once cursed Him" (240).

The reader of *Light in August* must be careful not to assume that these attitudes, characteristic of traditional Southern beliefs, are necessarily shared by Faulkner. There is a remarkable passage in the novel (in the opening pages of Chapter 19), in which Faulkner introduces the figure of Gavin Stevens, whose only role is to provide commentary about Joe Christmas. He also appears in some of Faulkner's other works, most characteristically as a commentator or "chorus." Since Gavin Stevens is a Harvard graduate and a district attorney, we might assume, quite mistakenly, that his reflections on Joe Christmas's behavior are objectively accurate and reflect the author's views. He gives a fascinating, if curious, account of Joe Christmas's last actions in terms of the "stain either on his white blood or his black blood. . . . the black blood drove him first to the negro cabin. And then the white blood drove him out of there, as it was the black blood which snatched up the pistol and the white blood which would not let him fire it. And it was the white blood which sent him to the minister. . . . And then the black blood failed him again, as it must have in crises all his life.

He did not kill the minister. . . . He crouched behind that overturned table and let them shoot him to death, with that loaded and unfired pistol in his hand" (424–25).

Stevens's explanation seems perhaps plausible at first reading. He accounts for a series of complex actions in a way that is highly articulate, and with just enough pseudo-psychology to sound authoritative. What is wrong with all of this is that, first, it is not at all clear that Joe has any black blood. Second, it is singularly unconvincing to attribute to the successive acts of a single person a genetic and racial explanation that is so literal; and indeed in this light the passage seems almost parodistic. Finally, the context of the actions surrounding Joe's death makes this explanation unintentionally ironic if we remember that Percy Grimm shoots Christmas (and worse) without compunction, and with no "black blood" to account for his deeds.[16]

It is important to examine Faulkner's fictional treatment of blacks if we wish to understand his own attitude. It occupies any number of his novels and stories, but here I am going to examine only the work, referred to earlier, in which Faulkner deals extensively and explicitly with blacks, Go Down, Moses (1942).

In this work, and especially in the famous novella "The Bear," the sympathetic protagonist, Ike McCaslin, describes what he believes to be the distinctive qualities of blacks: These are not the simplistic and violent qualities implied by Gavin Stevens. Ike says, "They are better than we are. Stronger than we are. Their vices are vices aped from white men or that white men and bondage have taught them. . . ."[17]

When challenged to name their virtues, Ike speaks first of "endurance," and then of "pity and tolerance and forbearance and fidelity and love of children" (294–95). It is only fair to point out that Ike McCaslin is as much as Gavin Stevens a fictional character who speaks and acts in specific fictional contexts, so that one must be careful in assuming that Faulkner's own beliefs are being presented. Nevertheless, the fact that Ike's actions are portrayed by Faulkner not only as admirable but as consistent with Ike's beliefs suggests a fundamental sympathy on the author's part. The great German author Goethe once declared (in *The Apprenticeship of Wilhelm Meister*) that to act is difficult; to think is more difficult still; but to act according to one's thought is the most difficult of all. Faulkner's treatment of Ike McCaslin pays tribute to this conception.

In *Go down, Moses* a number of short stories give clear and eloquent evidence of Faulkner's sensitivity not only to the abiding virtues of the blacks he portrays, but to the frequent ignorance of, or indifference to, these virtues in the white community. "Pantaloon in Black" is a moving story of a young black man named Rider, whose wife had died and whose consequent deep and inexpressible grief drives him to drink, and then to a dice game with his timber gang and one white man, the armed night watchman. Rider catches him using crooked dice, and the watchman reaches for his pistol. Rider kills him with a razor the moment before the gun fires. Rider is lynched in a nearby schoolhouse and the coroner takes all of five minutes to decree that Rider met his death "at the hands of a person or persons unknown." Later, the sheriff's deputy talks to his wife about Rider with staggering ignorance and insensitivity, even acknowledging that the watchman had been running a crooked game with the mill workers for 15 years. With impressive skill Faulkner is able to reveal the touching human grief of Rider that lies behind the narrative of the uncomprehending deputy. And something of the disparity between the actual inner life of Rider and the prejudiced or stereotyped ways in which he is seen by his society is obvious in the life of Joe Christmas.

In contrast to the recognitions of Ike McCaslin in "The Bear," Eupheus Hines and Percy Grimm and the townspeople of Jefferson will not, or cannot, see a black man as a person, or weigh his individual qualities. The moment Joe Christmas is labeled as a "Negro" he can no longer expect direct responses to his own being, but only the reactions that are determined by stereotype. Joe spends a lifetime struggling with the uncertainty of his identity, and with the confusing self-image that is the result of his internalization of stereotypes created by whites. His fellow men, however, need not struggle with such uncertainty about Joe; their attitudes, and their actions, are determined by the overriding category of "Negro." Rejected and defiant, Joe attempts to escape, and enters the "street which was to run for fifteen years" (210), the street that will not ever take him closer to identity, or community. Joe never finds an identity, either personal or social, with which he can live.

Faulkner's *Absalom, Absalom!* deals with the tragic story of Thomas Sutpen, who rejects his wife and repudiates his first son because he has discovered that his wife has some black blood. He had conceived a grand design—to create a great mansion and a dynasty that would save his own son from being insulted, as he had been as a poor boy in West Virginia. His intransigent repudiation of his wife and his son because they are part black lead to the destruction of his grand design. This compelling story can be read as a kind of legendary history of the American South. *Intruder in the Dust* is about a community's over-ready acceptance of the guilt of an alleged murderer primarily because he is black. He is innocent. In both cases it is clear that blacks are compelled to live according to the identities, and the code of behavior, imposed upon them by a white culture. I will have more to say about codes of conduct in the next chapter.

When Joe arrives in Jefferson at the age of 33, he has spent 15 years wandering (presumably from the time he abandons his foster home and is in turn abandoned by Bobbie Allen), a stranger and an exile from others, and from himself: "He thought it was loneliness which he was trying to escape and not himself. But the street ran on in its moods and phases, always empty: he might have seen himself as in numberless avatars, in silence, doomed with motion, driven by the courage of flagged and spurred despair; by the despair of courage whose opportunities had to be flagged and spurred" (213).

Three years later, he is in flight not only from himself, but from the pursuers who he knows will kill him if he is captured. There comes a moment made poignant by the suggestion that Joe, for all his complexities, has perhaps never wanted anything more than the life that Lena Grove represents: "It is just dawn, daylight: that gray and lonely suspension filled with the peaceful and tentative waking of birds. The air, inbreathed, is like spring water. He breathes deep and slow, feeling with each breath himself diffuse in the neutral grayness, becoming one with loneliness and quiet that has never known fury or despair. 'That was all I wanted,' he thinks, in a quiet and slow amazement. 'That was all, for thirty years. That didn't seem to be a whole lot to ask in thirty years' " (313).

But the life embodied by Lena, a life frequently and sympathetically depicted in Faulkner's work—at peace with itself, with humanity, and with nature—has been denied Joe.

We may remember the scene in Chapter 5 of the novel, when Joe spends an evening waiting for his final confrontation with Joanna Burden: "it seemed to him, sitting on the cot in the dark room, that he was hearing a myriad sounds of no greater volume—voices, murmurs, whispers: of trees, darkness, earth; people: his own voice; other voices evocative of names and times and places . . . which were his life, thinking *God perhaps and me not knowing that too* He could see it like a printed sentence, fullborn and already dead *God loves me too* like the faded and weathered letters on a last year's billboard *God loves me too*" (97–98).

Here too one has the poignant sense of other possibilities for Joe, in his momentary awareness that he belongs to life, is a part of the world of nature and of other people, a member of God's creation. But this sense of belonging and of acceptance is momentary only, "like a printed sentence . . . already dead," a message already faded like last year's billboard. He can imagine another mode of existence, but he is unable to shape this vision into a sustained way of life.

Now he is on the road to Mottstown, where he will stop running. Faulkner never explicitly accounts for Joe's decision to give himself up. Perhaps he is weary of flight, and of being pursued; perhaps he feels that this flight and pursuit are but a grotesque extension of a whole lifetime of flight. Perhaps the conditioning we have seen in the earlier episodes with the dietician and with McEachern force him to accept the idea of punishment that rightly follows transgression. On a Friday, one week after the murder of Joanna Burden, he approaches Mottstown, where he will be captured. " 'And yet I have been further in these seven days than in all the thirty years,' he thinks. 'But I have never got outside that circle. I have never broken out of the ring of what I have already done and cannot ever undo,' he thinks quietly . . . with before him the shoes, the black shoes smelling of negro: that mark on his ankles the gauge definite and ineradicable of the black tide creeping up his legs, moving from his feet upward as death moves" (321).

He dies as he has lived, an ambiguous and complex figure. His fate seems to us tragic, and yet he is not a traditional tragic hero. His violence and cruelty affect us simultaneously with his confusion and loneliness and victimization. He frightens us, and he demands of us a new kind of sympathy. He is not a hero, but he is not quite a villain. He is a victim: a figure regarded in traditional literary criticism as the object of pathos, rather than of tragedy. It is frequently felt in our time that human beings have no autonomy, no free will. They have been deprived of the ability to affect the circumstances that determine their lives. In consequence, the "victim" has become more and more often the protagonist of modern literature. Still, it can be argued that Joe Christmas refuses to be a passive victim only; he struggles with his destiny.

He is not necessarily black, although his society has decided that he must be. He is not necessarily white, nor can he ever decide whether he even wishes to be. He is, rather, a brilliantly realized representation of one kind of modern alienation. Even more than Gail Hightower or Joanna Burden, Joe Christmas is an outsider, unable to find any community in his circumscribed world. He suffers from, and fights against, the repressions of both a religious and a racial system. These systems are not written in stone, but reside more darkly in the minds of men. Faulkner makes us feel that while his tragedy is grounded in the particular milieu of the American South, Joe Christmas remains in our minds and memories as emblematic of universal human suffering.

12

Codes of Conduct

That human beings must live by some code—some value system or structure of belief—is one of Faulkner's recurring themes. In describing Faulkner as a novelist whose concerns are frequently moral and religious, one thinks of his continual examination of the codes by which his characters live, and his evaluations of the human behavior that stems from these codes. It should prove useful to consider here, however briefly, the codes that Faulkner deals with in his fiction. It has sometimes been assumed that Faulkner celebrated a single model: the code of honor, gallantry, and chivalry created in the South before the Civil War and debased by modernism. But a careful reading of Faulkner's fiction reveals a number of others. Although some of these codes overlap one another, each is still distinct. I indicate, by way of illustration, some of the works by Faulkner in which he examines these codes, but this is by no means an exhaustive list.

1. The traditional "Southern" code—of chivalry, honor, gallantry, bravery, and personal integrity. This code is important in many of Faulkner's works that deal with earlier history (*Sartoris, Absalom, Absalom! The Unvanquished*), and in some works in which

characters measure their modern lives or society against this code (*The Sound and the Fury*). Given its time frame, circa 1930, and its primary themes, *Light in August* does not deal with this code significantly, except perhaps ironically in Hightower's romantic dream-vision of his grandfather. But Hightower does not live by this code; it gives him none of the traditional qualities of honor, gallantry, or bravery. It is rather an escape from life: not a spur to action but to withdrawal.

2. The "hill-folk" or country-people code—of honest work, the acceptance of an organic or holistic relatedness to nature, gentleness, trust, native courtesy, and love. Clearly this is the code that governs the lives of Lena Grove and Bryon Bunch, and is celebrated frequently in Faulkner's other fiction, as in "The Bear."

3. The "black" code—already referred to in the discussion of *Go Down, Moses*—which includes "pity and tolerance and forbearance and fidelity and love of children." The absence of any direct representation of this code in *Light in August* is an ironic comment on Joe Christmas's racial ambiguity. It has been remarked that Faulkner's fiction generally avoided full-scale characterizations of blacks until he wrote *Go Down, Moses*.

4. A "timeless" code—essentially nonsectarian but religious; of self-transcendence, compassion, forgiveness, *caritas*. This code is memorably portrayed by Dilsey in *The Sound and the Fury*, and somewhat less convincingly by Nancy Mannigoe in *Requiem for a Nun*. It is the code by which Ike McCaslin wishes to live, and it is a large part of the thematic substance of *A Fable*. This is the code Hightower is tragically conscious of having betrayed by his fixation on violence and romantic gallantry, and perhaps the code toward which Joanna Burden strives in her work with blacks before Joe Christmas changes her life.

5. The code of "modernity"—of amorality, acquisitiveness, mechanistic lives and values, and rootlessness. This is the code of the famous Snopes tribe, and of Jason Compson in *The Sound and the Fury*. It can be argued that for Faulkner, modernity is not a code at all, but rather the absence of a code. It may be the absence of a code that allows for the rampant individualism and self-seeking that Faulkner portrays as characteristic of the twentieth century, and that contributes to the reduction of human life to mechanistic conceptions. For Faulkner, a characteristic of modernity—both literally and symbolically—is rootlessness, restlessness, or flight. This is most vividly illustrated

in the life of Joe Christmas, for the reasons already explained in the previous chapter. Lucas Burch is another good example, on a comic level, of many of the characteristics of modernity. Faulkner says of Burch that he is "just living on the country, like a locust" (33). He seduces Lena, and then runs away. He is Joe's partner in bootlegging, however incompetent, but he betrays Joe without compunction. Although he may have other motives for this betrayal, foremost among them is that he covets the reward money. Significantly, when we last see him he is running away again (perhaps with symbolic appropriateness, on an iron horse—the railroad train).

Like many other authors concerned with the representation of codes of conduct in modern literature, Faulkner is more likely to dramatize their betrayals rather than their fulfillments. It is clear from this summary that the tragic characters in *Light in August* are defined by their departures from ideal codes rather than by their willingness, or ability, to maintain them. Lena Grove's strength in the novel derives largely from her fidelity to the simple country-folk code. Byron Bunch also maintains much of this code, but his life is rather mechanical and over-regulated before Lena's arrival. It may be significant that his only friend seems to be the Reverend Gail Hightower, frozen in inaction, until his love for Lena pulls him away from Hightower and toward vital life. It is perhaps significant also that Byron's code is not overly rigid; once under Lena's influence he can sustain his love for her, although she bears another man's child.

Lena and, later, Byron are seen in contrast with Gail Hightower, who has betrayed the religious code that he realizes too late should have governed his life. Their lives can be contrasted also with that of Joe Christmas, who is deprived of any code at all by his society, and by his own inner conflicts. Since Joe falls outside of any known community, a victim of the worst kind of marginalization, he must make up his own isolated life as he goes along.

13

Faulkner: Technique and Style

It is both difficult and tempting to describe in a short space Faulkner's accomplishments as a writer. I shall begin by proposing a list of what seem to be the distinguishing elements of his fiction, and then go on to discuss at least some of these attributes, with substantial reference to *Light in August*.

The first four of these all have to do with Faulkner's remarkable inventiveness:

1. Great virtuousity in the innovative and experimental use of narrative and structural techniques.
2. Stylistic mastery of a wide range of voices.
3. Fecundity of imagination.
4. Largeness of vision.

To these should be added several others, which I discuss elsewhere in this volume. They are demonstrations of how technique and content can be bound together especially closely:

5. The creation of moral frameworks that both portray and evaluate human actions with a keen judgment that is tempered with compassion and humor.
6. The creation of a fictional world in which social and literary realism are enhanced, and sometimes transformed, by a legend-creating and myth-making imagination.

Faulkner was the most ambitious writer of fiction in the American twentieth-century. He was a deliberate and devoted craftsman of structure and style in the great tradition of Henry James and the British Joseph Conrad, both of whom he admired, and by whose high standards he wished to be judged. He was astonishingly versatile in his use of a wide range of narrative techniques; each of his novels represents some new departure in its technical attributes.

Faulkner used the techniques of stream of consciousness and interior monologue, which he had learned from James Joyce's *Ulysses*. But he did not merely imitate Joyce's technique; he transformed it for his own purposes. Faulkner used stream of consciousness more brilliantly and originally than any other American writer. At the same time, he broke with conventional chronology and made use of severe time dislocations. *The Sound and the Fury* unfolds in four sections, with four different narrators or centers of consciousness, each of whose stories is dramatized in a disarranged but thematically interesting chronology.

The first of the four sections is entitled "April 7, 1928" (which in that year was Easter Saturday, although Faulkner does not tell us this); the second, "June 2, 1910" (the day that Quentin Compson, this section's narrator, will commit suicide at Harvard); the third, "April 6, 1928" (Jason's section, related on Good Friday); and the fourth section, "April 8, 1928" (related by an unknown narrator again on Easter Sunday). Each section has an apparent autonomy of narration, but is in fact dependent on the other sections for either factual or interpretive completion. What seems at first a confusing discontinuity builds slowly to a narrative of remarkable richness.

Cumulatively these techniques engage the reader deeply in an emotional and intellectual involvement with a tragic history that is being re-created from the past. In the same way, when we read *Light in August* we have the illusion of collaborating with the author in the act of creation. This sense of re-creation is accomplished through the combined resources of memory (no great respecter of conventional chronology); and of delayed disclosure, which creates initially a sense of discontinuity. Narrative coherence is achieved by slow accretion, rather like a mosaic in which individual pieces have limited significance but which, when placed together, achieve an intelligible and beautiful form.

•   •   •

Added to these techniques are the tensions created by a variety of points of view or narrative perspectives, which we must both experience and evaluate in order to arrive at an understanding of the living past. The literal questions we may ask—What happened? How did it come about?—are immensely complicated and made richer by the dramatic representation of the very processes by which we experience and hope to understand history.

The traditional novels of the nineteenth-century tend to be narrated by an omniscient author who appears to control not only the narrative, but also the interpretation of its significance. (There are of course exceptions, such as the remarkable narrative voices of Emily Brontë's *Wuthering Heights*, which anticipates later narrative techniques.) Faulkner, following in the later tradition of impressionism employed by such authors as Henry James and Joseph Conrad, tends to present his narratives through the points of view of various characters within the plots of the story or novel. What is emphasized is the subjective responses of these characters to their experience (or perhaps one should say that "experience" is at least as much a matter of one's inner life as of objective events). What the reader understands as the meaning of fictional events comes in part from these particular points of view, which must be mediated—weighed and assessed, compared with other evidence, accepted or rejected—as part of the process of reading. As readers we have the illusion of creating meaning, of working toward interpretive understanding, much as we must in confronting reality. Our understanding of an event in the real world may be profoundly affected by what we know about our source of information. Our understanding and evaluation of a modern fictional narrative involves us in a similar process. Joe Christmas's life with his foster parents, for example, would be substantially different if this section of *Light in August* were to be recorded through the point of view of Simon McEachern. Such a change would affect not only the selection of scenes and episodes; it would materially alter our sense of the very significance of the plot.

In *As I Lay Dying*, Faulkner presents a story in a reasonably straightforward chronology, but in episodes of varying lengths, each of which is presented from a different point of view. Often the same material is repeated, but with the dramatically different perspectives of these varying viewpoints. On one level it is a comparatively "simple" narrative—the pilgrimage of a family transporting the coffin of the deceased wife and mother to Jefferson in fulfillment of her wish to be buried there. The adventures of the family along the way are inventive, if sometimes bizarre, and include variations on biblical themes of fire and flood. These events and the richness of characterization—achieved in large measure through the widely various narrative voices and perspectives that provide us with the "story"—elevate the novel to the stature of tragi-comic legend.

Absalom, Absalom! is even more directly concerned with the re-creation of history and the process of legend-making. Here Faulkner uses multiple voices and points of view in different and complex ways. A central narrator in the present, Quentin Compson of *The Sound and the Fury*, with the occasional aid of a sympathetic outsider, his Harvard roommate from Canada, pieces together the tragically violent history of the Sutpen family through what Quentin knows and what has been told to him by others. Some of these narrative sources present vivid but not necessarily reliable accounts, because they have had their own involvements in this history. Some of the material in this highly dramatic story—especially the significance and motivations of its characters—is only partially known and must remain speculative. Quentin Compson must piece these accounts together as best he can; the reader, in turn, must do the same. Our sense of the meaning of the novel is achieved eventually through the dramatization of the difficult struggles in which the narrators, and readers, engage themselves in order to arrive at the significance of a complex human drama.

In *Light in August* the narrative moves, as we have seen, from one story and its characters to another, sometimes with only the most tenuous links between them. Many nineteenth-century novels are structured with a number of plots and subplots, each involving some new characters. Such a novel, for example, is Dickens's *Bleak House*. But despite the presence of a large gallery of characters and subplots, the novel is organized firmly around a central core—the Courts of Chancery and the case of Jarndyce and Jarndyce. All of the elements in the novel play some contributory role in the unfolding of this central plot. But this is not quite the case in *Light in August*, in which we would be hard pressed to find a single narrative center.

In a very stimulating essay, Michael Millgate has suggested that a "model"—rather than a source—for this novel is Joseph Conrad's *Nostromo*, which presents a series of parallel lives in the portrayal of a whole social world. Here too the fictional material is presented from different perspectives, and the same episodes or incidents may be depicted from different points of view.[18] The analogy is useful and instructive. Yet *Nostromo* is essentially a novel that marks a transition between the traditional narratives of the nineteenth century and the modern novel. It is transitional in the sense that despite its impressionistic techniques and its manipulations of point of view, it is not so much unlike Dickens's *Bleak House*. *Nostromo* is still organized around a single narrative core: the silver mine of Costaguana, its history, and its powerful effects on the society and on the lives of a large number of individuals. Since no single narrative center dominates the structure of *Light in August*, we must seek some different principle of organization.

On one level, of course, it is the thematic material of the novel that connects its many stories. The impact of Calvinism on the lives of the characters; the alienation and marginalization of "outsiders"; and the racial tensions in this society provide a kind of thematic matrix that binds together the disparate stories. In addition, the setting of the novel—Jefferson in the earlier part of the twentieth-century—provides something of a unifying frame. But these unifying elements are not in themselves the formal or structural properties of the novel, or its narrative organization.

I have suggested in Chapter 5 that the fictional technique is one of juxtaposition—the placing of apparently unrelated, even strikingly contrasting, scenes or episodes side by side, without conventional transitions or connecting tissue between them. It is a technique deriving less from earlier novels than from twentieth-century poetry, most notably from T. S. Eliot's *The Wasteland* and (less important, I think, to Faulkner) the *Cantos* of Ezra Pound. Faulkner was most certainly familiar with *The Wasteland*, influences of which can be seen, for instance, in *The Sound and the Fury* (as well as in other novels of the era such as Hemingway's *The Sun Also Rises* and Fitzgerald's *The Great Gatsby*). The technique of juxtaposition requires considerable agility on the part of the reader, and an active collaboration in combining the immediately available and powerful emotional effects with intellectual understanding. Readers of *Light in August*, as well as of *Wasteland*, frequently respond strongly to the emotional power of the work before they necessarily "understand" its techniques and modes of organization.

Many of the episodes in *Light in August*, especially in the earlier part of the novel, deal with actions that are incomplete, or with actions the significance of which is not revealed to us until much later.[19] Thus, a burning house is pointed out to Lena Grove as she arrives in Jefferson, but she (and we) can have no way of understanding its possible significance. We move rapidly to Byron Bunch, who remembers the much earlier appearance of Joe Christmas in Jefferson, as well as of Lucas Burch–Joe Brown. But there is no account of how Joe Christmas may relate to this fire, or Brown to Lena Grove. When we do learn more about Joe Christmas (and therefore his possible connection with the fire), as well as the true identity of Joe Brown as Lucas Burch (and hence his connection with Lena), it is indirectly, through a conversation with yet another new center of narrative interest, the Reverend Gail Hightower. His own story, in turn, is only partially disclosed, and its possible relationship to the other narrative threads remains unclear for some time.

We move then without transition to Joe Christmas, who is presented on the evening before the murder of Joanna Burden. This episode is intensely dramatic, but with only the faintest of clues about what we are to make of him, either in terms of his character or of his present actions. Then we have another sharp transition in which the past of Joe Christmas is represented. This history is given at great length in a straightforward chronological sequence, and occupies some seven chapters of the work, almost as though a new novel were beginning. Through these chapters we come to understand a great deal about Joe Christmas, although I think it fair to say that our feelings toward him are kept in a somewhat precarious ambivalence.

When the novel resumes its account of present action, the narrative technique of delayed disclosure is continued so that our understanding of the characters is often held in suspense for long periods. Hightower is introduced in Chapter 3, but a full revelation of why he has remained in Jefferson is withheld until the penultimate chapter of the novel. Christmas's vigil on the eve of Joanna Burden's murder is vividly portrayed long before we know what has happened between her and Joe Christmas that will lead to its bloody termination. Finally, it is not until fairly late in the novel (Chapter 16) that we learn about the circumstances of Christmas's birth and Eupheus Hines's actual relationship to him as his grandfather. I have commented earlier on the uncertainty attached to a number of elements in the story. But there are still other questions that remain unanswered: Does Hightower die at the end of his grim encounter with self-knowledge? Is Joe Christmas's real father a Mexican or part black? Does Joe Christmas actually kill his foster father?

The present action of the novel (with the exception of the last chapter, which is somewhat indeterminate) takes place over 11 days, from a Friday, when we first meet Lena on the road, to a Monday, when Joe Christmas is captured and killed.[20] But in the course of the novel these 11 days are bound by countless narrative threads to the entire lifetimes of the major characters, and sometimes even to the lives of parents and grandparents. This continuous weaving of the past into the present tends to make everything in the novel seem dramatically *present*, rather than being an extended chronicle of several generations of social and personal history, as we are accustomed to finding in more traditional "family" novels such as John Galsworthy's *The Forsythe Saga* or Thomas Mann's *Buddenbrooks*. This narrative technique is singularly appropriate to the themes of the novel, in which the importance of the past is the way it continually impinges on and conditions present actions.

Earlier I discussed the variety of styles Faulkner uses in the opening chapters of the novel. Here it is enough to point out that Faulkner's command of folk vernacular is among the most convincingly authentic in American literature. Faulkner is in the company of Mark Twain in his sensitivity to speech rhythms and his ability to re-create a living oral language. It is through his careful recording of this vernacular that we are given, without comment, the wonderful sense of natural courtesy and civility that runs through the relationships of "simple" country people. This dignified and kindly courtesy may be seen in the conversations between Lena and the Armstids, for instance, or in Byron Bunch's dealings with Hightower.

The ease and naturalness of Faulkner's vernacular can be seen in the dialogues of Lena and Bryon, or in the episode when Lena stays with the Armstids:

> "I would like to help," Lena says.
> Mrs. Armstid does not look around. She clashes the stove savagely. "You stay where you are. You keep off your feet now, and you'll keep off your back a while longer maybe."
> "It would be a beholden kindness to let me help."
> "You stay where you are. I been doing this three times a day for thirty years now. The time when I needed help with it is done passed." She is busy at the stove, not back-looking. "Armstid says your name is Burch." (14)

While there may be disagreement about the last chapter of the novel, there can be none about the authenticity of the furniture dealer's extended monologue:

> So there he was skirmishing around, getting camp ready, until he got me right nervous: him trying to do everything and not knowing

just where to begin or something. So I told him to go rustle up some firewood. . . . I was a little mad, then, at myself about how I had got into it now and I would have to sleep on the ground with my feet to the fire and nothing under me. . . . Then he came back, with enough wood to barbecue a steer. . . . Then we had it, sho enough. It was like those two fellows that used to be in the funny papers, those two Frenchmen that were always bowing and scraping at the other one to go first, making out like we had all come away from home just for the privilege of sleeping on the ground. (473)

Earlier in the novel there is a wonderful passage in which the Jefferson millhands discuss the new worker who calls himself Joe Brown:

Mooney said: "Well, Simms is safe from hiring anything at all when he put that fellow on. He never even hired a whole pair of pants."

"That's so," Byron said. "He puts me in mind of one of these cars running along the street with a radio in it. You can't make out what it's saying and the car ain't going anywhere in particular and when you look at it close you see that there ain't even anybody in it."

"Yes," Mooney said. "He puts me in mind of a horse. Not a mean horse. Just a worthless horse. Looks fine in the pasture, but it's always down in the spring bottom when anybody comes to the gate with a bridle. Runs fast, all right, but it's always got a sore hoof when hitching-up time comes."

"But I reckon maybe the mares like him," Byron said.

"Sho," Mooney said. "I don't reckon he'd do even a mare any permanent harm." (32–33)

In the midst of so much tragic history in this novel, Faulkner can present wonderfully humorous and sardonic vignettes of ordinary life when it is caught up in extraordinary events, as in the splendid descriptions of the sheriff's frustrating use of bloodhounds to pursue Joe, from which I quote only one section:

They ran side by side for a hundred yards, where they stopped and began to dig furiously into the earth and exposed a pit where someone had buried recently emptied food tins. . . . For a short time the dogs moiled, whimpering, then they set off again, full-tongued, drooling, and dragged and carried the running and cursing men at top speed back to the cabin, where, feet planted and with backflung heads and backrolled eyeballs, they bayed the empty doorway with the passionate abandon of two baritones singing Italian opera. The men took the dogs back to town, in cars, and fed them. When they crossed the square the church bells were ringing, slow and peaceful, and along the streets the decorous people moved sedately beneath parasols, carrying Bibles and prayerbooks. (280–81)

The sense of welcome for any novelty or diversion in lives that are otherwise dull or commonplace is nicely captured in the description of Jefferson's new firetruck at the scene of the newly discovered murder of Joanna Burden. But what makes it especially memorable is Faulkner's awareness of how the innocence of novelty can also turn quite sinister:

[The fire truck] was new, painted red, with gilt trim and a hand-power siren and a bell gold in color and in tone serene, arrogant, and proud. About it hatless men and youths clung with the astonishing disregard of physical laws that flies possess. It had mechanical ladders that sprang to prodigious heights at the touch of a hand, like opera hats; only there was now nothing for them to spring to. It had neat and virgin coils of hose . . . but there was nothing to hook them to and nothing to flow through them. So the hatless men, who had deserted counters and desks, swung down. . . . They came too and were shown several different places where the sheet had lain, and some of them with pistols already in their pockets began to canvass about for someone to crucify. (272)

Faulkner's style can range from the vernacular and the humorous to great eloquence, compounded of high rhetoric, elaborate sentence structures, and intense passages of emotionally charged description and imagery. His sentence structures are sometimes extremely extended and intricate. At their worst they may demand a number of bemused readings before their basic sense becomes clear, and one must ask, "What is being modified?" or "What is the referent of these far-removed pronouns?" Even when his sentences are not so convoluted they can still give pause, as with this example in which Hightower is brooding about Protestant church music: "It was as though they who accepted it and raised voices to praise it within praise, having been made what they were by that which the music praised and symbolized, they took revenge upon that which made them so by means of the praise itself" (347).

The style can take on a lyrical quality, resulting partly from Faulkner's sensitivity to sentence rhythms and alliteration, and partly from a "poetic" use of run-in descriptive words. There are many such words in *Light in August*, like "daygranaried" (55), "thwartfacecurled" (164), "softungirdled" (219), and "flabbyjowled and darkcaverneyed" (290).

Faulkner often employs a sustained and recurring imagery that is not merely decorative, but also interpretive. Lena's pilgrimage is undertaken on country roads with slow curves and low hills; Joe Christmas's pilgrimage is on city streets with harsh linearity. Many of the Joe Christmas episodes take place at night; Hightower's crucial moments come at dusk; Lena is seen almost always in daylight.

Hightower's moment of tragic recognition is described through the recurring image of an inexorable wheel (of memory), caught in sand (forgetfulness and repression), but relentless in momentum once it starts to move. And reference has already been made to the recurring image of the urn, with its Keatsian associations of serenity and timeless perfection (and sometimes of lifelessness).

Even names can take on suggestive emotional overtones in *Light in August*. "Hightower" suggests a spire, but also a lofty removal from ordinary life, and from the proper work of the church; he is a "professional who has removed the bells from its steeples" (461). "Christmas" has obvious religious associations, but with some rather ambiguous wrenchings of those associations. "Grimm" is an appropriate name for the ruthless National Guardsman, and may also be suggestive of the Brothers Grimm, famous for their violent and ferocious tales. "Burden" has obvious associations, already referred to, with the stern and joyless Puritan view of mortal human life; Joanna's family also includes a "Calvin," as a kind of thematic underlining; and a "Nathaniel," which may be a passing glance at Hawthorne, the great fictional chronicler of American Puritanism. "Grove" conveys pleasant associations with mild and nurturing nature; while "Lena" is a customary shortening of "Magdalen," which has its own religious overtones. "Bobbie Allen" bears a sardonic allusion to the old English folk song of unrequited love, "Barbara Allen." And Lucas Burch borrows his new name, Joe Brown, from a once-famous film comedian whose most distinguishing feature, besides general inanity, was a very large mouth.

The very title of the novel calls attention to itself as an image or metaphor. A frequent assumption about this title is that it refers to the country idiom about a pregnant woman's time of delivery; and indeed Lena Grove gives birth to her child in August. Such an interpretation is made, for instance, by Malcom Cowley.[21] But Faulkner has insisted on another explanation of the title's origin: "in August in Mississippi there's a few days somewhere about the middle of the month when suddenly there's a foretaste of fall, it's cool, there's a lambence [sic], a luminous quality to the light, as though it came not from just today but from back in the old classic times. It might have fauns and satyrs and the gods and—from Greece, from Olympus in it somewhere. . . . Maybe the connection was with Lena Grove, who had something of that pagan quality of being able to assume everything, that's—the desire for that child, she was never ashamed of that child whether it had any father or not."[22]

Frequently Faulkner's style is sonorous and portentous, registering the presence of a bemused and brooding intelligence pondering the follies and misfortunes of finite human beings. Thus, when Byron Bunch comes to rouse the sleeping Hightower because he is needed to assist at the birth of Lena's baby, the author pauses in the midst of what might have been narrated as a simple action. Faulkner seems to step back from this moment in order to meditate on its embodiment of all human frailty and vulnerability: "He [Byron] approached the bed. The still invisible occupant snored profoundly. There was a quality of profound and complete surrender in it. Not of exhaustion, but surrender, as though he had given over and relinquished completely that grip upon that blending of pride and hope and vanity and fear, that strength to cling to either defeat or victory, which is the I-am, and the relinquishment of which is usually death. Standing beside the bed Byron thought again *A poor thing. A poor thing"* (372).

This effect of brooding meditation, which is in a sense timeless, and which interrupts or "freezes" the action, is reinforced by the heavy use of abstract nouns: *surrender, pride, hope, vanity, fear, defeat, victory, death.*

Faulkner's style can be weighted with heavily charged language, much in the manner of Joseph Conrad in such a work as *The Heart of Darkness.* On the same page as the quotation I cited on Protestant church music (347), there appear the following words: *sonorous, abjectness, solemn, profound, stern, implacable, immolation, catastrophe.* It can of course be argued that these words are appropriate to the subject; but what is distinctive is the insistent repetition of effect and its cumulative power. One is struck by the heavy weight assigned to language itself, as distinct from action or characterization, or even of an imagery that might communicate feeling or emotion without quite so much explicit verbal direction.

This style of high rhetoric, of elaborated sentence structures, and of brooding compassion is rarely as excessively mannered in *Light in August* as it can sometimes be in Faulkner's other writing, especially in his later works. Its effects are several: It creates and sustains an atmosphere of human misfortune and suffering, which is so much of the novel's burden. It raises the story above the level of empty violence and sensationalism, which might otherwise easily be taken as the object of the novel. It invests this particular story, involving particular people, with a sense of a larger, almost cosmic, significance. Here, as elsewhere in Faulkner's work, Jefferson is a small town in Mississippi, and at the same time is everywhere human beings live and aspire and suffer.

14

The Lena Grove Story: Ending

The last chapter of *Light in August* has been the object of considerable critical disagreement. Here Faulkner leaves the tragic worlds of
Joe Christmas and Gail Hightower and returns to the world of Lena
Grove, in which the novel began. But while the opening of the novel
is recorded from the point of view of a "concealed" narrator, recording action and dialogue more or less objectively, the last chapter
is reported by a first-person narrator, an unnamed furniture dealer
who makes his first and only appearance here. Why has Faulkner
introduced a new point of view to report indirectly on Lena Grove's
continued pilgrimage, attended by the dogged Byron Bunch? One
school of criticism maintains that this last chapter brings the novel
back down from its high pitch of tragic violence to the continuing
cycle of "normal" human life: romantic love, marriage, child-rearing.
Faulkner does this in a comic mode, perhaps imitating the ancient
Greek tradition of following a tragedy with a satyr play. The satyr
plays were frequently "Dionysian," or broadly sensual, in marked
contrast to the high style and serious import of the tragedies that
preceded them.

Another school of criticism regards the ending of *Light in August* as an artistic mistake—an excessively coy or "cute" treatment of Lena and Byron, accompanied by the mildly titillating suggestion that the narrator is engaged in sexual byplay with his own wife as he tells her about Byron's puppy-dog devotion to Lena, who keeps him firmly, if not necessarily finally, in his place. In a curious way, this conclusion to *Light in August* is similar to the last chapters of *The Adventures of Huckleberry Finn*, also controversial because of its farcical and demeaning schemes to let the black slave Jim escape when he is already free. The analogy is a suggestive one, but only in a limited way. The conclusion of *Light in August* does not really affect our understanding of Joe Christmas or Gail Hightower, but the conclusion of *Huckleberry Finn* does affect our understanding of the relationship between Huck and Jim.

Two issues are involved here. One, which I will deal with first, concerns the basic story of Lena Grove and Byron Bunch, the story with which the novel ends.

The furniture dealer's story does not, after all, deny or cancel the tragic passions of the earlier narrative so much as it puts them in balance. The tragic vision dramatized in the body of the novel as it deals with the lives of Christmas and Hightower is tempered by the comic vision that insists on the simultaneous reality of the lives of Lena Grove and Byron Bunch.

The world of Yoknapatawpha County is a tragic world: It contains human beings whose lives are terrible, whether through their circumstances or their own human failings. But Yoknapatawpha County, which is Faulkner's microcosm of the world, also includes characters capable of human love, of simple dignity, of continuity. We need to remember that Hightower, called upon to act as midwife to Lena, finds himself called back to the human community. At home again and resting, he muses: "*She will have others, more* remembering the young strong body from out whose travail even there shone something tranquil and unafraid. *More of them. Many more. That will be her life, her destiny. The good stock peopling in tranquil obedience to it the good earth; from these hearty loins descending mother and daughter*" (384).

Byron Bunch also represents a figure looking forward to a richer life of human love and fulfillment. Although he is one of the very few characters in the novel whose past is not revealed, we know enough about his present life before Lena enters it. He is dominated by a work ethic that leads him to spend most of his days at the mill, scrupulously accounting for every interval of rest or relaxation. He works overtime on Saturdays; rides many miles to preach at country churches on Sundays; and returns to Jefferson to start the long week again. While all of this is exemplary, it does seem an escape from personal involvement, less dramatic than Hightower's, but equally effective. At the end of the novel we see him freed: He is in love, with the same dogged persistence as earlier he had given to his work routine, but with new springs of passion and involvement. And when Hightower thinks of the good stock peopling the good earth, he knows that Lena's next children will be Byron's as well (384).

There is a similar balancing of vision in Tolstoy's *War and Peace*. After all the harrowing experiences of the Napoleonic invasion of Russia, the suffering and deaths, and the disappointments in the lives of many of the characters, the conclusion of Tolstoy's novel shows the central characters persisting in what he suggests is the primary cycle of human life: falling in love, getting married, and raising children who, in turn, fall in love. . . . Interestingly, some critics and readers have objected also to Tolstoy's conclusion, finding it excessively anticlimactic, domestic, or bourgeois.

The critical disagreement about these novels' conclusions is no doubt in part an aesthetic one, stemming from one's sense of the form and consistency of a literary work. But the disagreement also may involve issues and values that go beyond the aesthetic, touching on our own sense of what is most meaningful about human life.

The second issue involved in the conclusion of *Light in August* is more directly related to a technical or aesthetic problem. We may grant that it is altogether fitting that Faulkner balances the tragedies of the main body of the novel with the happier possibilities in the story of Lena Grove that frames the novel. Still, I confess to some uneasiness about a certain "cuteness," a sniggering tone in the style of the concluding narration, which makes the affirmations of the Lena-Byron story a bit difficult to accept:

> I begun to notice how there was something funny and kind of strained about [Byron]. Like when a man is determined to work himself up to where he will do something he wants to do and that he is scared to do. I don't mean it was like he was scared of what might happen to him, but like it was something that he would die before he would even think about doing it if he hadn't just tried everything else until he was desperate. That was before I knew. I just couldn't understand what in the world it could be then. And if it hadn't been for that night and what happened, I reckon I would not have known at all when they left me at Jackson.
>
> *What was it he aimed to do?* the wife says.
>
> *You wait till I come to that part. Maybe I'll show you, too.*
> (471–72)

Why must this narration be presented through the agency of the furniture dealer? Perhaps the answer is that there is some problem in the reader's acceptance of Lena Grove as a convincing and important figure in the scheme of the novel. She may seem to many readers *too* simple and naive, too bland or "primitive." She is perhaps too narrowly limited in her embodiment of femininity—whether or not she is intended to be an emblem of the feminine principle—to be believable as a character, or to be a sufficiently convincing counterweight to the worlds of Joe Christmas and Gail Hightower. The creation of the furniture dealer, however, may serve to establish that the world of Lena Grove and Byron Bunch *does* exist. The furniture dealer is himself part of this world, which he authenticates through his idiom and style of narration, his amused but sympathetic attitude toward Lena and Byron, and his own amiable sexuality. Just as at the beginning of the novel the Armstids understand Lena completely, and deal with her with the manners belonging to her world, so at the end does the furniture dealer function in the same way. Whether this is a sufficiently convincing argument that offsets the "cuteness" of the novel's ending is, of course, a matter of continuing debate. As readers of the novel, you will want to be part of this ongoing discussion.

APPENDIX: NOBEL PRIZE ACCEPTANCE SPEECH

I feel that this award was not made to me as a man, but to my work—
a life's work in all the agony and sweat of the human spirit, not for
glory and least of all for profit, but to create out of the materials of
the human spirit something which did not exist before. So this award
is only mine in trust. It will not be difficult to find a dedication for the
money part of it commensurate with the purpose and significance of
its origin. But I would like to do the same with the acclaim, too, by
using this moment as a pinnacle from which I might be listened to by
the young men and women already dedicated to the same anguish and
travail, among whom is already that one who will some day stand here
where I am standing.

Our tragedy today is a general and universal physical fear so long
sustained by now that we can even bear it. There are no longer problems of the spirit. There is only the question: When will I be blown
up? Because of this, the young man or woman writing today has
forgotten the problems of the human heart in conflict with itself, which
alone can make good writing, because only that is worth writing about,
worth the agony and the sweat.

He must learn them again. He must teach himself that the basest
of all things is to be afraid; and, teaching himself that, forget it forever,
leaving no room in his workshop for anything but the old verities and
truths of the heart, the old universal truths lacking which any story
is ephemeral and doomed—love and honor and pity and pride and
compassion and sacrifice. Until he does so, he labors under a curse.
He writes not of love but of lust, of defeats in which nobody loses

anything of value, of victories without hope, and, worst of all, without pity or compassion. His griefs grieve on no universal bones, leaving no scars. He writes not of the heart but of the glands.

Until he relearns these things, he will write as though he stood among and watched the end of man. I decline to accept the end of man. It is easy enough to say that man is immortal simply because he will endure; that when the last ding-dong of doom has clanged and faded from the last worthless rock hanging tideless in the last red and dying evening, that even then there will still be one more sound: that of his puny inexhaustible voice, still talking. I refuse to accept this. I believe that man will not merely endure: he will prevail. He is immortal, not because he alone among creatures has an inexhaustible voice, but because he has a soul, a spirit capable of compassion and sacrifice and endurance. The poet's, the writer's, duty is to write about these things. It is his privilege to help man endure by lifting his heart, by reminding him of the courage and honor and hope and pride and compassion and pity and sacrifice which have been the glory of his past. The poet's voice need not merely be the record of man; it can be one of the props, the pillars to help him endure and prevail.

—William Faulkner
Stockholm
10 December 1950

NOTES AND REFERENCES

Literary and Historical Context

1. James Linn and W. T. Taylor, "Counterpoint: *Light in August*," in *A Foreword to Fiction* (New York, 1935), 144–57.

2. Harry Campbell and Ruel Foster, *William Faulkner: A Critical Approach* (University of Oklahoma Press, 1951).

3. S. D. Woodworth, *William Faulkner en France* (Paris, 1959).

4. George Marion O'Donnell, "Faulkner's Mythology," *Kenyon Review* I (Summer, 1939), 285–99.

5. Malcolm Cowley ed., *The Portable Faulkner* (New York: Viking Press, 1946).

6. Joseph Blotner, *Faulkner: A Biography* (New York: Random House, 1974).

7. Granville Hicks, *The Great Tradition: An Interpretation of American Literature Since the War* (New York: Macmillan, 1933), 265–68.

8. Irving Howe, *William Faulkner: A Critical Study* (New York, Random House, 1952; revised edition, 1975).

A READING

1. Randall Stewart, *American Literature and Christian Doctrine* (Baton Rouge: Louisiana State University Press, 1958), 136–42.

2. William Faulkner, *Light in August* (New York: Modern Library College Edition, 1968), 9; hereafter cited in text.

3. *Faulkner in the University*, eds. F. L. Gwynn and J. Blotner (Charlottesville: University of Virginia Press, 1959), 74. Hereafter cited in text.

4. Regina Fadiman, *Faulkner's Light in August: A Description and Interpretation of the Revisions* (Charlottesville: University of Virginia Press, 1975).

5. See Harold J. Douglas and Robert Daniel, "Faulkner's Southern Puritanism," in *Religious Perspectives in Faulkner's Fiction* ed. J. Robert Barth (Notre Dame: Notre Dame University Press, 1972), 37–51.

6. *The Faulkner-Cowley File*, ed. Malcom Cowley (New York: Viking Press, 1966), 31–32.

7. Joseph Blotner, *Faulkner: A Biography* (New York: Random House), 110, 160, 784.

8. Victor Hugo, *Les Miserables*, trans. Charles Wilbour (New York: Modern Library, n.d.), 245. I am indebted to Jayne Berland for pointing out this passage to me.

9. See Warren Beck, "William Faulkner's Style," in *William Faulkner: Three Decades of Criticism* eds. F. Hoffman and O. Vickery (East Lansing: Michigan State University Press, 1960), 143.

10. See J. P. Sartre, "Time in Faulkner: *The Sound and the Fury*," in Hoffman and Vickery, 225–32.

11. See W. R. Moses "The Unity of *The Wild Palms*," in *Modern Fiction Studies* II (Autumn 1956), 125–31.

12. Gwynn and Blotner, 72.

13. Gwynn and Blotner, 86.

14. Gwynn and Blotner, 72.

15. Myra Jehlen, *Class and Character in Faulkner's South* (New York: Columbia University Press, 1976), 89–90.

16. When asked while in residence at the University of Virginia about the significance of Gavin Stevens's surmises, Faulkner replied: "That is an assumption, a rationalization which Stevens made. That is, the people who destroyed him made rationalizations about what he was." Gwynn and Blotner, 72.

17. *Go Down, Moses* (New York: Modern Library, n.d), 294.

18. See Michael Millgate, " 'A Novel: Not an Anecdote': Faulkner's *Light in August*" in *New Essays on Light in August*, ed. Michael Millgate (Cambridge: Cambridge University Press, 1987), 41–42. Hereafter cited in text.

19. A fuller and excellent account of intertwining actions in the novel will be found in Martin Kreiswirth, "Plots and Counterplots: Faulkner's *Light in August*," in Millgate (1987).

20. See Stephen E. Meats, "The Chronology of *Light in August*," in *The Novels of William Faulkner: Light in August*, ed. Francois Pitavy (New York: Garland Publishing, 1982), 227–35.

21. Malcolm Cowley, *The Portable Faulkner* (New York: Viking Press, 1946) 652.

22. Gwynn and Blotner, 199.

SELECTED BIBLIOGRAPHY

Primary Works

This listing of published volumes does not include collections edited by others during or after Faulkner's lifetime. Books cited are novels unless identified otherwise.

The Marble Faun Poetry. Boston: Four Seas, 1924.

Soldier's Pay. New York: Boni & Liveright, 1926.

Mosquitoes. New York: Boni & Liveright, 1927.

Sartoris. New York: Harcourt, Brace, 1929. *Flags in the Dust*, the earlier rejected version, was published posthumously in 1973.

The Sound and the Fury. New York: Cape & Smith, 1929.

As I Lay Dying. New York: Cape & Smith, 1930.

These Thirteen (Stories). New York: Cape & Smith, 1930.

Sanctuary. New York: Cape & Smith, 1931.

Light in August. New York: Smith & Haas, 1932.

A Green Bough (Poetry). New York: Smith & Haas 1933.

Doctor Martino and Other Stories (Stories). New York: Smith & Haas, 1934.

Pylon. New York: Smith & Haas, 1935.

Absalom, Absalom. New York: Random House, 1936.

The Unvanquished. New York: Random House, 1938.

The Wild Palms (with *Old Man*). New York: Random House, 1939.

The Hamlet. New York: Random House, 1940.

Go Down, Moses (Stories and Novella). New York: Random House, 1942.

Intruder in the Dust. New York: Random House, 1948.

Knight's Gambit (Stories). New York: Random House, 1949.

Collected Stories of William Faulkner. New York: Random House, 1950.

Requiem for a Nun. New York: Random House, 1951.

A Fable. New York: Random House, 1954.

Big Woods. New York: Random House, 1955.

The Town (Part of trilogy, following *The Hamlet*). New York: Random House, 1957.

The Mansion (Third volume of trilogy). New York: Random House, 1961.

The Reivers. New York: Random House, 1962.

Secondary Works

Interviews, Speeches, Letters, and Essays

Fant, Joseph L. and Robert Ashley, eds., *Faulkner at West Point.* New York: Random House, 1964.

Jelliffe, Robert A., ed., *Faulkner at Nagano.* Tokyo: Kenkyusha, 1956.

Meriwether, James B., ed., *Essays, Speeches and Public Letters.* New York: Random House, 1966.

Meriwether, James B. and Michael Millgate, eds., *Lion in the Garden: Interviews with William Faulkner, 1926–1962.* New York: Random House, 1968.

Watson, James G., *Thinking of Home: William Faulkner's Letters to His Mother and Father, 1918–1925* (New York: Norton, 1992).

Biographies

There are many biographical studies, as books or parts of books; listed here are full-length biographies.

Blotner, Joseph. *Faulkner: A Biography.* 2 vols. New York: Random House, 1974.

Coughlan, Robert. *The Private World of William Faulkner.* New York: Harper & Brothers, 1954.

Minter, David. *William Faulkner: His Life and Work.* Baltimore: Johns Hopkins University Press, 1980.

Oates, Stephen B. *William Faulkner: The Man and the Artist.* New York: Harper & Row, 1987.

Selected Bibliography

Critical Studies

There are now innumerable critical studies of Faulkner's work. For a fuller listing, consult the following:

Bassett, John. *Faulkner: An Annotated Checklist of Recent Criticism*. Kent: Kent State University Press, 1983.

McHaney, Thomas L. *William Faulkner: A Reference Guide*. Boston: G.K. Hall, 1976.

Meriwether, James. B. "Faulkner," in *Sixteen Modern American Authors*, ed. Jackson A. Bryer (Durham: Duke University Press, 1974) 223–75.

Books

Adams, Richard P. *Faulkner: Myth and Motion*. Princeton: Princeton University Press, 1968. Good insights on individual novels; less persuasive as a general study than other studies.

Barth, J. Robert. *Religious Perspectives in Faulkner's Fiction: Yoknapatawpha and Beyond*. Notre Dame: Notre Dame University Press, 1972. A stimulating collection of essays on religious themes in Faulkner's fiction.

Beck, Warren. *Man in Motion*. Madison: University of Wisconsin Press, 1961. One of Faulkner's earlier, and soundest, critics.

Bedell, George C. *Kierkegaard and Faulkner: Modalities of Existence*. Baton Rouge: Louisiana State University Press, 1972. Seeks parallels between Kierkegaard's Christian existentialism and Faulkner's themes.

Brooks, Cleanth. *William Faulkner: Toward Yoknapatawpha and Beyond*. New Haven: Yale University Press, 1978. A quite substantial study, with occasionally controversial readings.

Davis, Thadious M. *Faulkner's Negro: Art and the Southern Context*. Baton Rouge: Louisiana State University Press, 1982. A study of Faulkner's fictional treatment of blacks, as well as his public pronouncements on racial issues.

Guerard, Albert J. *The Triumph of the Novel: Dickens, Dostoevsky, Faulkner*. New York, Oxford University Press, 1976. A stimulating comparative study, without close readings of individual novels; controversial commentary on Faulkner's alleged misogyny.

Hoffman, Frederick and Olga Vickery, eds. *William Faulkner: Three Decades of Criticism*. East Lansing: Michigan State University Press, 1960. A very useful collection of published articles on general themes and techniques, and on individual works.

Howe, Irving. *William Faulkner: A Critical Study*. Third revised edition Chicago: University of Chicago Press, 1975. A revised edition of one of the earlier—and better—introductions to Faulkner's fiction.

Jehlen, Myra. *Class and Character in Faulkner's South.* New York, Columbia University Press, 1976. A sociological study, not always sensitive to the particularities of the fiction.

Kerr, Elizabeth M. *William Faulkner's Yoknapatawpha.* Revised edition. New York: Fordham University Press, 1985. A thematic discussion and analysis of recurring patterns and themes in Faulkner's fiction.

Kreiswirth, Martin. *William Faulkner: The Making of a Novelist.* Athens: University of Georgia Press, 1983. One of the best of the more recent studies of Faulkner's fiction.

Millgate, Michael. *The Achievement of William Faulkner.* London: Constable, 1966. Among the very best of the book-length studies of Faulkner, with excellent material on Faulkner's manuscripts as well as on various sources and influences.

———, ed. *New Essays on Light in August.* Cambridge: University of Cambridge Press, 1987. A good collection of articles, mainly fairly recent ones, on various aspects of the novel.

Pitavy, Francois. *Faulkner's "Light in August."* Bloomington, Indiana University Press, 1973. Sensitive and perceptive analysis of the novel.

———. *William Faulkner's Light in August: A Critical Casebook.* New York: Garland, 1982.

Pilkington, John. *The Heart of Yoknapatawpha.* Jackson: University of Mississippi Press, 1981. A rather general survey of the Yoknapatawpha legend.

Stonum, Gary Lee. *Faulkner's Career: An Internal Literary History.* Ithaca: Cornell University Press, 1979.

Vickery, Olga. *The Novels of William Faulkner.* Baton Rouge: Louisiana State University Press, 1964. One of the earlier, and still useful, studies of Faulkner's fiction.

Waggoner, Hyatt H. *William Faulkner: From Jefferson to the World.* Louisville: University of Kentucky Press, 1959. Especially useful for its treatment of the moral frameworks of Faulkner's fiction.

Weisberger, Jean. *Faulkner and Dostoevsky: Influence and Confluence.* Trans. Dean McWilliams. Athens: Ohio State University Press, 1974. A comparative study of possible influences and thematic resemblances.

Williams, David. *Faulkner's Women: The Myth and the Muse.* Montreal: McGill-Queens University Press, 1977. A stimulating study of a controversial subject: Faulkner's fictional treatment of women.

Selected Bibliography

Articles:

Benson, Carl. "Thematic Design in *LIA*." *South Atlantic Quarterly* 53 (October 1954): 540–55.

Berland, Alwyn. "*Light in August*: The Calvinism of William Faulkner." *Modern Fiction Studies* 8 (Summer 1962): 159–70.

Bleikasten, Andre. "Fathers in Faulkner." In *The Fictional Father: Lacanian Readings of the Text*, ed. Robert Con Davis (Amherst: University of Massachussets Press, 1981), 115–46. Attempts a psychoanalytical interpretation of family relationships.

Collins, R. G. "*Light in August*: Faulkner's Stained Glass Triptych." *Mosaic* 7 (Fall 1973): 97–157.

Cottrell, Beekman W. "Christian Symbols in *LiA*." *Modern Fiction Studies* 2 (1956–57): 207–13.

Gwynn, Frederick L. "Faulkner's Raskolnikov." *Modern Fiction Studies* 4 (1958–59): 169–72. A comparative study of Dostoevsky and Faulkner.

Hungerford, Harold. "Past and Present in *Light in August*." *American Literature* 55 (1983): 183–98.

Kazin, Alfred. "The Stillness of *Light in August*." *Partisan Review* 24 (Autumn 1957): 519–38. Reprinted in *William Faulkner: Three Decades of Criticism* 247–65. An influential study of the novel, with some emphasis on style and tone.

Lind, Ilse Dusoir. "The Calvinistic Burden of *Light in August*." *New England Quarterly Review* XXX (September 1957): 307–29.

———. "Faulkner's Uses of Poetic Drama." In *Faulkner, Modernism, and Film*, eds. E. Harrington and A. J. Abadie (Jackson: University Press of Mississippi, 1979), 66–81.

Longley, John L., Jr. "Joe Christmas: The Hero in the Modern World." In *The Tragic Mask* (Chapel Hill: University of North Carolina, 1963), 192–205.

Maddex, Jack P. "Postslavery Millenialism: Social Eschatology in Antebellum Southern Calvinism." *American Quarterly* 46 (1979): 46–62.

Moses, W. R. "The Unity of *The Wild Palms*." *Modern Fiction Studies* II (Autumn 1956): 125–31. Although primarily concerned with another work, this article has stimulating comments on Faulkner's treatment of sex and love.

Petesch, Donald A. "Faulkner on Negroes: The Conflict between the Public Man and the Private Art." *Southern Humanities Review* 10 (1976) 55–64.

Phillips. K. J. "Faulkner in the Garden of Eden." *Southern Humanities Review* 19 (1985) 1–18.

Sandstrom, Glenn. "Identity Diffusion: Joe Christmas and Quentin Compson." *American Quarterly* 19 (1967) 207–23. A psychological study of theme of personal identity.

Tritschler, Donald. "The Unity of Faulkner's Shaping Vision." *Modern Fiction Studies* V (1959–60): 337–43.

Tucker, John. "William Faulkner's *Light in August*: Toward a Structuralist Reading." *Modern Language Quarterly* 43 (June 1982): 138–55. A reading of the novel in terms of recent critical theory.

Zink, Karl E. "Faulkner's Garden: Women and the Immemorial Earth." *Modern Fiction Studies* II (Autumn, 1956): 139–49. Thematic study of eternal feminine themes.

Index

THE AUTHOR

Alwyn Berland is the author of *Culture and Conduct in the Novels of Henry James* (Cambridge: Cambridge University Press, 1981), and of the chapter on Henry James in the volume *American Literature* in the *New Pelican Guide to English Literature* (Harmondsworth: Penguin, 1988). He has published many articles on literary criticism in Great Britain and the United States, and short stories in Canada and the United States. He was the founder of the *Wascana Review* and its editor from 1965 to 1969.

He is presently professor emeritus of English and the former dean of Humanities at McMaster University. At McMaster he was chairman of the Board of Management, and then managing editor, of the Bertrand Russell Editorial Project. He served as the executive secretary of the Canadian Association of University Teachers from 1968 to 1973. In 1988–89 he was visiting professor of English at Nanjing Normal University in China.